TURNING THE TABLES ON
RESTAURANT ECCLESIOLOGY

Chris Brockway

God bless you
Crispian

Cris.

...with grateful thanks to my family
and my church family
for allowing the space and time
to wrestle all that's captured in this book.

Contents

Introduction	01
Chapter 1	Restaurant Ecclesiology	06
Chapter 2	History Informing The Present	17
Chapter 3	Socio-Psychological Explorations	38
Chapter 4	Commitment and Covenant	59
Chapter 5	Family Table Ecclesiology	76
Conclusion	95
Appendix A	Summary of Covenants In The Old Testament	98
Appendix B	Etymological Methodology For *'Koinocovenantal Commitment'*	103
Bibliography	108

TURNING THE TABLES ON
RESTAURANT ECCLESIOLOGY

Introduction

Having been in church leadership for more than two decades, I often contemplate the complexities of primarily organising the local church around a three-fold trajectory towards what I would argue to be God-given priorities of spiritual growth, numerical growth and augmented missional engagement. Appropriately, our practice in the local church is necessarily human-resource dependent, profoundly relational and principally voluntary. My hyperbolised analogous conclusion is that much of the time, the contrasting experience for both leaders and congregation is akin to life in a metaphorical restaurant.

Based primarily upon my personal experience of two decades leading local churches and my own anecdotal accounts and that of other church leaders, my metaphorical 'customers' decision to frequent our 'restaurant' oftentimes appears to be unreservedly determined by their personalised and particular preferences. For example, attendees will conscientiously consider the type of 'cuisine' served, having first conducted online research paralleled to reading reviews on Trip Advisor, alongside off-line research amongst friends and family. Then, like a broadsheet critic, if all of the above is deemed satisfactory, from arrival until the point of departure, heuristic judgements will be inaudibly made for better or worse. This initial critique might include the location, ease of parking, quality of hospitality, standard of facilities to entertain children, and overall ambience, etc.

Ultimately, however, such matters are secondary to concerns around the excellence of the analogous 'food and drink' served. 'Customers' sit down at a 'table,' most often amongst the individual(s) they came with (or at least with others like them) and, although subliminally aware of the other 'tables' contributing to the overall atmosphere, the majority of 'customers' are not seeking to engage proactively with anyone beyond their group.

From beginning to end, such is the culture of many a local church, 'customers' expect excellent service, anticipating that the 'restaurant' will serve their preferred menu choices to meet their exacting and bespoke preferences. When the 'customer' departs, subject to feeling well-fed, they may become loyal repeat customers who frequent, alongside other satisfied customers, until such time standards fluctuate, their tastes alter or 'the management' changes. If 'the customer' is episodically left wanting or dissatisfied, they reserve the right to leave, generally without causing perspicuous offence or enmity, concluding that their experience is undeserving of repetition or no longer gratifying their specific and variable tastes.

Whilst such a description is without doubt hyperbole to make a specific point, the leadership experience is equally reminiscent of a restaurant, albeit conversely from a serving rather than consumeristic perspective. For example, staff and ministry teams invest inordinate amounts of time making preparations, seeking to eliminate any hinderances whatsoever to customers experiencing outstanding hospitality. 'Managers' persistently worry about online and offline critique and then, from the moment 'the customer' arrives, like restaurant waiting-staff, ministry teams figuratively dash from table to table, seeking to understand and gratify the multifaceted requirements of the different groups, rarely unifying the disparate 'diners' gathered.

Throughout, the 'front of house' experience is incessantly perfected while seeking to contain multidimensional governance intricacies beyond public view. Succinctly stated and somewhat unwittingly, our single-minded ministry philosophy can become the safeguarding of customer loyalty and upholding tradition while pioneering new ideas, in the hope of extending this excellent customer-focused service to new 'diners' so that the whole enterprise has sustainable growth year after year, alongside a distinguished reputation worthy of the brand's founder.

Such a focus might be an excellent strategy for a restaurant, but is it sincerely befitting of the church of Christ? Is such an approach even satisfactorily meeting the spiritual and relational needs of the majority of the congregation? What place is there for confrontation, rebuke and challenge, since, ultimately, the priority of leadership ought to be pleasing God, not people (Gal.1:10)? Are these symptoms of contemporary culture, and to what extent should we be obliging them?

Contained within the pages of this book is an imperfect attempt, (and it is imperfect), to explore the extent to which church membership, and more specifically covenant commitment, can be an effective tool to reorientate the church, especially the under 50s, towards a healthier expression of commitment.

Chapter 1 explores and contrasts the differing 'pre-' and 'post-SAGA' generation(s) relationship with the local church, specifically highlighting differing levels of generational commitment.

In Chapter 2, historical perspectives to contemporary practice are considered, specifically exploring church membership in the early church and the foundational, covenantal basis for membership compared to contemporary expectations.

Socio-psychological influences upon contemporary practice are highlighted in Chapter 3, revealing a disparity between current societal values and the historical and theological conclusions of Chapter 2.

Chapter 4 further explores the significance of covenantal theology in the founding ecclesiology, specifically of the Baptist Church (of which I am a part), identifying the Scriptural/theological basis of covenants, before proposing a new phrase, '*koinocovenantal commitment.*' Although describing Baptist perspectives, the insights shared are equally applicable to any denominational or non-denominational context.

The coining of '*koinocovenantal commitment'* is an attempt to redeem an authentic understanding of covenant within a proposed new ecclesiological model, 'Family Table Ecclesiology,' described in Chapter 5.

In conclusion, I argue that church membership is an effective tool to nurture commitment, especially amongst the under 50s. However, if it is to effectually counter postmodern values of individualisation, consumerism, commitment phobia, anti-authoritarianism and the homogenising effects of globalisation, this tool needs to be sharpened, calibrating it within historical and theological understandings of covenant-commitment.

1 | Restaurant Ecclesiology

The description of the consumerist church in the Introduction is unmistakably a caricature and not one intended to cause offence, but it is an oversimplification nonetheless based upon the authentic experience of many church leaders. In fact, this experience extends beyond gathered worship to all areas of church life. As McLaughlin argues, the use of such figurative descriptions can be helpful to identify and resolve problems: 'some of the deepest truths [of the Bible] are metaphorically expressed.'[1] Consequently, for the sake of identifying and resolving the problem, I have metaphorically labelled this mode of church 'Restaurant Ecclesiology'.

At worst and most cynically expressed, Restaurant Ecclesiology is an exhausting, frequently frustrating, and ostensibly impoverished, romanticised, translation of the healthy experience described in Scripture, despite the early church's inherent interpersonal, doctrinal and moral quandaries (e.g. Ac.2:42-46; cf. Ac.5:12, 11:1-18). At best, whilst sympathetic to societal contemporary pressures upon members, Restaurant Ecclesiology feels like a relentlessly repetitive travail generating inadequate

---

[1] Rebecca McLaughlin, *Confronting Christianity: 12 Hard Questions for the World's Largest Religion* (Wheaton: Crossway, 2019), 95.

solutions to ever-enduring questions.

Are we not supposed to eat around one table rather than sit in small, sub-cultural, groups around multiple tables...? In response, some might argue "...at least we are all in the same restaurant even if we are sitting at different tables!" but, is that enough? Was this actually Jesus' vision for his church? Is there a more copacetic model of ecclesiology which has congruence with Christ's vision? We sing 'Come to the table, all are welcome here'[2] but to which table (or tables) are we inviting people to eat? Are we one synergised and covenanted Body or several bodies awkwardly co-habiting? Does our table even represent something attractive or more importantly, reflective of Biblical principles? Is 'consumerism Christianity' and such acquiescent leadership even Scriptural?

My conviction is that there must be a more effective model than Restaurant Ecclesiology, especially if we are to effectually nurture Christ-like commitment within the life of the church. Traditionally, especially within our Baptist context, Membership[3] (however formalised) has been the principal tool to both substantiate and unambiguously demonstrate such commitment.[4] However, primarily amongst the pre-SAGA (<50s) generations,[5] Membership is proving to be a progressively ineffective tool. While the pre-SAGA generation(s) are contented to become Members by name, in nature this membership is increasingly

---

[2] Dave Frey, Ben Glover, Ben McDonald, *Come to the Table*, Warner/Chappell Music, Inc, Capitol Christian Music Group, Universal Music Publishing Group.
[3] The model and history of Baptist Church Membership will be explored further in Chapter 2.
[4] The history of the Baptist Church will be explored in Chapter 2.
[5] A definition of the 'SAGA generation' and a comparison with the pre-SAGA generation(s) is offered below.

expressed in a consumeristic, non-contributive fashion. To be fair, notable exceptions to this generalisation are those already working or volunteering in leadership positions of intensely people-focused organisations/institutions. Thus, our challenge is encouraging the pre-SAGA generation(s) to become predominantly more than consumers.

Defining the 'SAGA Generation'

The so-called SAGA generation is satirically referred to as the 'Mick Jagger generation.' The label 'SAGA generation' is argued to have been coined following a Church Army conference entitled 'SAGA Church,' focused on fresh expressions of work with older people.[6]

This group assiduously challenge negative stereotypes around ageing. Born after World War 2, their parents were responsible for post-war repopulation, causing this combined pre-senior and senior group to be labelled the 'baby-boomers.' In the 1960s, this generation were optimistic teenagers, subsequently becoming counter-cultural activists later that same decade. Now they are commonly considered to be young-old, working active and/or retired independent computer-literate persons. They are a time-rich group with disposable income, exercising significant political and economic influence, bringing about contemporary change as 'grey warriors.'[7]

At least 50% of this generation have church backgrounds,

---

[6] Michael Collyer, 'What Church For The SAGA Generation? Cultural shifts in the younger old,' Church Army: *"Discovering Faith in Later Life,"* issue 6 (March 2007), 3.

[7] Amy Hanson, *Baby Boomers and Beyond: Tapping the Ministry Talents and Passions of Adults over Fifty*, Leadership Network (San Francisco: Jossey-Bass, 2010), 3–18.

albeit the majority have become de-churched.[8] The SAGA generation who remain connected with more institutional forms of contemporary church do so with spiritual incongruity, however. Comfort and security are found in such association, yet this generation resolutely contributes, partially motivated by a reminiscent spiritual yearning for something more.

The SAGA generation is fuelled by their participation, or at least observation of, and collective memory of the cross-denominational charismatic renewal which began in the early 1960s. This renewal promoted an approach to faith characterised by increased activism and ever-increasing Spirit-empowered participation.[9] Consequently, resolute commitment is embedded in the SAGA generations' ecclesiological DNA which the pre-SAGA generation have never experienced. Brown rather depressingly argues this group, who grew up in a culture of rational scientific confidence and an increasingly secular worldview, were the generation who pioneered the beginning of the death of Christian Britain (modernity), becoming the first generation to enter the post-Christendom (post-modernity) era.[10]

In the UK, SAGA Magazine capitalised upon this group's disposable income and adventurous attitude through targeted marketing of holidays and financial products tailored to their needs. Subsequently, a burgeoning new movement emerged which has gotten beyond ageist-witticisms to become an esteemed badge of honour. The SAGA generation constitutes the committed core of many,

---

[8] Michael Collyer, 'What Church For The SAGA Generation? Cultural Shifts in the Younger Old,' *Crucible: The Journal of Social Ethics* (April-June 2008), 4-12.
[9] For more detail, see David William Bebbington, *Evangelicalism in Modern Britain: A History from the 1730s to the 1980s* (London: Unwin & Hyman, 1995), 227-246.
[10] Callum G. Brown, *Postmodernism for Historians* (Harlow: Pearson, 2005), 3–11.

if not most local church communities.

The table below, based upon very broad brushstroke observations, highlights the contrasting generational approaches to membership:

pre-SAGA generation(s) < 50 years	SAGA-generation >50 years
Consumers	Contributors
Those Served	Those Serving
The Led	The Leaders
Receivers	Givers
Passive	Active
Partial-Hearted	Wholehearted
Participation Optional	Participation Prioritised
Spectating	Participating
'Me' Focussed	'We' Focussed
Associative	Participative
Commitment-Phobic	Covenantally-Committed
Fringe-Stakeholders	Invested-Stakeholders
Membership is a 'Grind'	Membership is a 'Gift'
Less Engaged in Spiritual Disciplines	More Engaged in Spiritual Disciplines
Re-active in Exercising Spiritual Gifts	Pro-active in Exercising Spiritual Gifts

Table 1: Contrasting Generational Approaches to Church Membership

As highlighted above, engagement by the pre-SAGA generation(s) is enduringly commitment-phobic, resulting in sporadic attendance at Members' Meetings and perpetuating a vague disinclination to exercise natural, spiritual and grace gifts.[11] By contrast, the SAGA generation are stronger, based on their own testimony, in engaging with spiritual disciplines and exercising spiritual gifts. My contention is that this disparity is the primary symptom contributing to the dis-ease of Restaurant Ecclesiology.

More specifically within my experience of Baptist ecclesiology, the SAGA-generations' expression of commitment is considered functionally healthy while the pre-SAGA generation(s) commitment is judged dysfunctional, especially for those opting to become Members.[12] The most articulated reasons for such commitment-resistance centre around poverty of time and finance. However, such excuses seem disingenuous since, if necessary, both the purse strings and the diary can be liberated, even at short notice, if deemed necessary (e.g. attending a party, purchasing a new gadget, etc.). Are these challenges unique to 21st century believers or have previous generations wrestled with similar impediments?[13]

Understanding Ecclesiology

Ecclesiology is the combining of two Greek words, 'ekklēsia' (church/assembly) and '-logia' (words, knowledge or logic) to mean 'the study of the church.'[14] After various historic

---

[11] Further socio-psychological consideration of the trends identified within our local context will be further explored in Chapter 3.

[12] A definition of appropriate commitment will be offered in Chapter 2.

[13] Further discussion of these themes will follow in subsequent chapters.

[14] Lorelei F. Fuchs, *Koinonia and the Quest for an Ecumenical Ecclesiology: From Foundations through Dialogue to Symbolic Competence for Communionality* (Grand Rapids: William B. Eerdmans Pub. Co, 2008), 6–7.

terminological shifts, 'ecclesiology' now delineates various ways the church defines and subsequently structures itself, which is inevitably a tension between historical continuity and progressive vision for the future.[15] Consequently, ecclesiology develops over time, having conscientiously weighed biblical texts, doctrines, and traditions, alongside adequate consideration of contemporary events and long-term vision(s). Ecclesiological formation, however, does not happen in isolation from other factors affecting people and their lives.

We Baptists, for example, have just such a distinct and systematic free-church ecclesiology, conditioned by socio-psychological factors which can and do, rightly or wrongly, alongside our traditions and models of governance, impede our previously stated three-fold trajectory of growth.[16]

Baptist-believers affiliate themselves with the universal church,[17] expressing that commitment through membership of local churches.[18] More specifically, Baptists espouse an independent congregationalist polity[19] with practice prioritising commitment to the Bible, a Trinitarian doctrine and emphasis on believers' baptism.[20] Such polity is essential because, at least in the first instance,

---

[15] See Horz Balz and Gerhard Schneider, *Exegetical Dictionary of the New Testament,* vol. 1 (Grand Rapids: Eerdmans, 1990), 410.

[16] Socio-psychological factors affecting ecclesiology will be considered in Chapter 3. Our three-fold trajectory of growth was defined in the Introduction.

[17] By 'universal church,' I mean it adheres to the four distinctive marks of traditional Christian ecclesiology: 'one, holy, catholic and apostolic' as expressed in the Nicene Creed.

[18] The history, practice and theology of Baptist Church Membership will be considered further in Chapter 2.

[19] Paul S. Fiddes, *Tracks and Traces: Baptist Identity in Church and Theology,* Studies in Baptist History and Thought 13 (Eugene, OR: Wipf and Stock, 2006), xvi.

[20] The Baptist Union of Great Britain, *Article 1 of the Declaration of Principle,* accessed July 09, 2019, www.baptist.org.uk/Publisher/File.aspx?ID=216696.

it establishes the church,[21] defining its particular distinctive to which individuals subscribe, and the wider body corporately and constitutionally uphold.[22]

As Feucht,[23] Luther,[24] Hammett[25] and Garret[26] argue, there is no organisational hierarchy within Baptist ecclesiology, underpinned by a theological understanding of the priesthood of believers (1.Pe.2:9). Significantly, Garett's understating includes a vertical (God-ward) and horizontal (other person-ward) commitment which, as I will elucidate in Chapter 4, is an essential characterising distinction. Hammett advances three indispensable criteria for Membership within a Baptist context: regenerate conversion, believer's baptism, and acceptance of the church's covenant, before subsequently arguing that membership 'is not only a status; it is an office'[27] thus advancing my understanding that membership is understood better as a verbed (dynamic) noun.

Within Baptist ecclesiology therefore, our constitutions and more tangibly our regular Members' Meetings, at least in theory and idealistically, ensure governance is not only the task of ordained ministry but equally the responsibility of every Member. Baptist churches are therefore a

---

[21] Mark Dever, Jonathan Leeman, and James Leo Garrett, *Baptist Foundations: Church Government for an Anti-Institutional Age* (Nashville: B&H Publishing Group, 2015), 3.

[22] Mark Dever, Jonathan Leeman, and James Leo Garrett, *Baptist Foundations*, 4.

[23] Oscar E. Feucht, *Everyone a Minister: A Guide to Churchmanship for Laity and Clergy* (St. Louis: Concordia Pub. House, 1994), 64.

[24] See George G. Hunter, *Church for the Unchurched* (Nashville: Abingdon Press, 1996), 121.

[25] John S. Hammett, *Biblical Foundations for Baptist Churches: A Contemporary Ecclesiology* (Grand Rapids: Kregel Publications, 2005), 146-150.

[26] James Leo Garrett, *Baptist Theology: A Four-Century Study* (Macon: Mercer University Press, 2009), 134.

[27] John S. Hammett, *Biblical Foundations for Baptist Churches*, 353.

Christocracy (a body of believers or Christocrats, expressed through membership, governed by the living, resurrected Jesus) not a Democracy (discerning the majority mind and will of the people). As Barth argued, 'True church law arises from hearing the voice of Christ as attested in Scripture.'[28]

Authority is vested in the church as a whole, whereby members (1) select, appoint, and, if necessary, remove church leaders; (2) help guard pure doctrine; (3) exercise church discipline and decide on membership; (4) participate in significant decisions affecting the entire congregation.[29] It is within this fourth area where the previously referenced commitment-absenteeism of the pre-SAGA generation(s) is problematic since their Christocratic-voice is deficient and, arguably, their membership is less effective than expected or constitutionally mandated. Readers from other denominational persuasions will straightforwardly be able to make equivalent application to their context.

The undesirous outcome in our Baptistic context, and wider within the Baptist Union based upon personal observation, is an uncorroborated two-tier membership comprised of fringe members (predominantly the <50s) and participant members (predominantly the >50s). So-called fringe members undoubtedly have the regenerate beliefs of Christianity without dilution, but, generally speaking, they abdicate from the additional responsibilities that participant membership stipulates. Fringe members measure their commitment by attendance on Sundays and,

---

[28] Karl Barth, G. W Bromiley, and Thomas F Torrance, *Church Dogmatics. Volume IV, Part 2, Volume IV, Part 2,* (Edinburgh: Bloomsbury Publishing, 2000), 682.
[29] James Leo Garrett, *Baptist Theology: A Four-Century Study* (Macon: Mercer University Press, 2009).

in the majority of cases, small group involvement. Significantly, without personal contention, the majority of fringe members absent themselves from Members' Meetings and are imperceptibly represented at a leadership level. If they do serve within ministries, it is likely, albeit arguably, because such service is meeting their own needs rather than by virtue of altruistic motives.

The pre-SAGA generation(s)' participation is optional and determined by a consumer mentality where they use the church as a service provider (like a subscription-based gym); it is, therefore, their right to 'exercise' based upon personal motivation and/or other life influences. Ward contends that this fashions an ever-downward, mutually destructive, vicious spiral: as members lessen commitment, leaders, consciously or subconsciously, attenuate their expectations to accommodate such modernist values.[30]

Employing a different metaphor, Leeman argues that such association, where one impersonally treats the church like a petrol station where we transitorily go to fill up our tanks, will eventually cause believers to have a misshapen, one dimensional (vertically-focused only) Christianity.[31] Leeman's thesis is supported by my previously stated anecdotal experience amongst the under 50s, who are generally lacking in horizontal commitment even if their vertical, God-ward commitment, is sincere.

This rather bleak, albeit hyperbolised analysis, begs the question: why are we experiencing a commitment problem,

---

[30] Peter Ward, *Liquid Church*. (Eugene: Wipf & Stock Publishers, 2013), 17–20.
[31] Jonathan Leeman, *The Church and the Surprising Offense of God's Love: Reintroducing the Doctrines of Church Membership and Discipline*, IX Marks (Wheaton: Crossway Books, 2010), 22.

what Leeman calls 'an ecclesiological mess,'[32] in our contemporary expression of church, especially since our inherited model of congregational governance has served us and our forebears well historically? If, as Pelikan suggests, the 20th century was the period within which ecclesiology in its broadest understanding evolved to become mature,[33] how does our ecclesiology need to function differently to aide further maturation? Regardless, is further maturation, in reality, little more than fossilisation of an antediluvian model requiring a radical revolution?

To answer these questions, before proposing a new paradigm to supersede Restaurant Ecclesiology (chapter 5), I will consider whether the problem is ecclesiological (chapter 2); a socio-psychological worldview conflict (chapter 3); or a theological problem with our understanding/implementation of membership? (chapter 4).

---

[32] Jonathan Leeman, *The Church and the Surprising Offence of God's Love,* 31–32.
[33] Jaroslav Pelikan, *The Christian Tradition 5: Christian Doctrine and Modern Culture since 1700*, The Christian Tradition 5 (Chicago: University of Chicago Press, 1989), 22.

2 | History Informing The Present

As argued in Chapter 1, ecclesiology is intrinsically a development of a church's traditional, doctrinal and circumstantial roots. 'In its contemporary manifestation, Christianity is to a significant degree the product of the historical circumstances and forces that have shaped it. It is, in short, a tradition.'[34]

For example, in my current local church context, there has been 150 years of antecedent and formative local ministry (tradition) and over 400 years of denominational history which is itself a disputatious repercussion of broader church history. Consequently, our ecclesiology has ineluctable continuity with enduring historic causative effects and thus cannot be disregarded when considering the validity of contemporary practice: 'You have to know the past to understand the present.'[35]

Membership can variously be evaluated: theologically, juridically, and sociologically. The theological approach, which will be emphasised in this chapter, originates from

---

[34] Stanley J. Grenz and John R. Franke, *Beyond Foundationalism: Shaping Theology in a Postmodern Context* (Louisville: Westminster John Knox Press, 2001), 94.
[35] C.E.Sagan, cited in J. Michael Adams and Angelo Carfagna, *Coming of Age in a Globalized World: The Next Generation* (Bloomfield: Kumarian Press, 2006), 288.

biblical foundations. Accordingly, I will compare our contemporary hopes for membership with biblical interpretations and historic denominational expectations.

Membership In A Local Church Context

In Baptist circles, we grandiosely describe membership as 'one of the most fulfilling aspects of a person's Christian walk,' further stating that Membership 'properly understood...tangibly expresses [1] our commitment to Christ and also [2] our commitment to other believers.' Purposefully, the vertical (God-ward) and horizontal (other-ward) commitment is accentuated. In consonance with our denominational heritage and contemporary constitutional constraints, membership is conditional upon: (1) persisting regenerate conversion to Christ; (2) assurance of serving and living under the authority of Christ as mediated through the local church; and in some local churches (3) believer's baptism. Benefits of membership are inextricably connected to responsibilities which include: regularly attending church services, prayer meetings and Members' Meetings; seeking the mind of Christ; supporting the vision of the church; to love, to pray for and to encourage others; giving to the work and vision of the church; and living in a way which is honouring to God in service to him and to each other.

These responsibilities, furthermore, tangentially communicate our desire for community engagement through the exercising of natural, spiritual and grace gifts, be that internally (when gathered) or externally (when scattered). Membership is privately substantiated, publicly affirmed and corporately corroborated.

The above précises how, at least in our Baptist world, we

imperfectly endeavour to tangibly determine the spiritual and/or commitment health, or otherwise, of an actual or aspirant member. Conspicuously in most Baptist churches, our practice negates any requirement for a signed covenant between members and the church,[36] only requiring verbal assent, through interview, of the aforementioned '2Cs' before bureaucratic form-filling for data collection, legislative consent and written confession of the candidate's regenerate faith. However, is such practice historically and theologically sound or sufficient evidence of regeneration and commitment, even if a pragmatic necessity?

As we shall see below, the onward trajectory of Baptist ecclesiology claims to be initiated by, and founded upon, pioneering convictions established around biblical interpretations, provoked by dissatisfaction with the controlling status quo propagandised by the state church.

Before considering the socio-psychological factors affecting ecclesiological dynamics relating to membership (chapter 3), which Healy contends are influential since such consideration avoids idealised abstraction,[37] my purpose here is to identify how 'membership' (or at least its principles) have been historically interpreted and practised. This analysis is crucial since, as Morris argues, 'ecclesiology should be founded on what is revealed in Scripture about how God, as Father, Son and Spirit, relates to the church.'[38]

---

[36] Reasons for abandoning a signed covenant will be explored in chapter 4.

[37] Nicholas M. Healy, *Church, World, and the Christian Life: Practical-Prophetic Ecclesiology*, Cambridge Studies in Christian Doctrine (Cambridge: Cambridge University Press, 2000), 25-51.

[38] Helen Morris, *Flexible Church: Being the Church in the Contemporary World*, (London: SCM Press, 2019), 63.

My primary focus will be upon New Testament records of the early church in Acts, alongside a brief consideration of Pauline teaching which theologises and evolves early practice. Old Testament references will be considered in chapter 4 when exploring the biblical role of covenants.

Church Membership In the New Testament

Acts is insightful, revealing how the church 'belonged' to one another. What follows are Scriptures which seem helpful in seeking to understand the early church's concept of 'membership.'

The first thing to unambiguously state is that there is no explicit reference to formalised 'membership' in Acts or the Scriptures generally. Similarly, nowhere is there a prescribed ecclesiology. Scripture, as I will demonstrate, contains various descriptions of what the church 'did' but does not explicitly detail the 'how.' For example, Scripture describes 'the body of Christ' (Ro.12:5; 1 Cor.12:12–27; Eph.3:6, 5:23; Col.1:18, 24) without detailing exactly how this 'body' was to be arranged, which was perhaps intentional in order that each church, at any time in history or place geographically, could organise themselves contextually. Scripture reveals how the church from infancy, comparatively free and unstructured, developed its ecclesiology contextually to become increasingly reliant upon organisational systems to sustain its mission and ministry, which, at least speculatively, may have included some form of 'membership' roll.

'Membership' In Acts

Acts 2:42-47 is often heralded as 'the blueprint,' which the contemporary church should aspire to replicate, at least in principle. These new believers met daily to worship, pray and learn, albeit there is no evidence of any structured, institutionalised organisation. There is, however, evidence of a defined, and head-counted group, as we read that people were 'being added to it' (Ac.2:27). While not a formalized system of membership, there implicitly appears to be an unsubstantiated membership, of sorts, by association, which encouraged participative commitment as a tangible expression of a believer's commitment to God and others (cf. Ac.4:32-37).

As the early church grew, primary forms of ecclesiological organisation similarly arose, as evidenced by Acts 5:12-14. Believers begin to meet, albeit temporarily before being scattered in Acts 8, as a pragmatic logistical necessity, at Solomon's Colonnade. Josephus describes this area as being substantial and contained: 'There was a porch without the temple...supported by walls of four hundred cubits, made of four-square stone...the length of each stone was twenty cubits, and the breadth six.'[39] The church had, for the first time recorded, corporately congregated beyond, and probably in addition to, the homes of individuals (cf. Ac.2:45).

When scattered, homes were again utilised; so, the use of Solomon's Colonnade is by no means a prooftext for 'megachurches' being a preeminent biblical model (cf. Col.4:15; 1 Cor.16:19; Rom.16:5). As the Scriptures reveal, under threat of persecution, people thought twice before being linked with the church (Ac.5:12-13). Here we see the first tangible signs that the defining mark of belonging to the group was 'believing' which preceded the possibility of

---

[39] Henry St J. Thackeray, and Flavius Josephus, *Books I-III*, Reprinted, Josephus Jewish Antiquities, 5 [1] (Cambridge: Harvard Univ. Press, 2001).Volume I. 20. c. 8. sect. 7.

subsequent 'joining.'

Acts 6 chronologically reveals that, in line with Baptist conviction, the church is constituted by regenerate believers, albeit there is no indication at this point how the early church decided who were the 'true believers' or how they prohibited unbelievers participating, if indeed they did. Verses 2-3 record what might be considered the first members' meeting, to deal with practical problems concerning the organisation of their ministry.

Following persecution, Acts 8 marks a paradigm shift for the church when it becomes trans-local. Aside from references to the Apostles in Jerusalem, and interventions from proficient itinerant leaders like Peter and John, there are no signs yet as to how this dispersed church is organised or how people belong to it. However, Saul initiates persecution towards an unambiguous group of believers in Damascus by referring to them as 'Followers of the Way' (Ac.9:2, 22:4). Such a distinction would suggest that this is an identifiable group although no indication is given of how or what constituted belonging. While this might reflect belonging by association, perhaps these are signs of more formalised belonging with, at the very least, a list of names akin to an elementary 'membership' roll.

Defined congregations, especially family-like house churches, in specific geographical contexts, continue to be identified throughout the New Testament (e.g. Corinth, Ephesus, Philippi, etc.), which leads me to conclude that individuals were gathering regularly and 'belonging' within the same groupings, within an evolving trans-local ecclesiological systemisation sustaining their ministry. Pointedly, in support of this thesis, when converted, Saul attempted to 'join' the disciples in Jerusalem (Ac.9:26).[40] The Greek word used, translated 'join' (*kollao*), means 'to glue or cement oneself to' which denotes mutual consent and enduring covenantal agreement. The same word is used in Matthew 19:5 of a man being 'joined' to his wife; in Luke 15:15 of the prodigal son contractually 'joining himself' to a firm of pig breeders; and in Acts 5:13 where outsiders did not 'join' the church. The strength of the word 'join' should, therefore, be understood as a marriage-like depth of relationship, which surpasses mere rudimentary spatial association.[41]

As news of Saul's conversion spread, it is evident from the gossip (Ac.9:21-26) that distinction could be made between the regenerate and unregenerate: "Isn't this the same man who persecuted Jesus' followers with such devastation in Jerusalem?" (Ac.9:21). There is still no evidence of an institutionalised church with formalised membership but there is increasing evidence of qualified belonging, what Baptists have called 'the church of visible saints' (e.g. Barnabas testifies to Saul's regenerate faith which permits him to 'join' or 'be glued to' them, Ac.9:27-30).

The only 'entry' point into the church mentioned is through belief in and obedience to Christ with the outward act of baptism being the public and most visible sign, but this

---

[40] Galatians 1:18 indicates that Paul's attempt to be wholly joined to the church had to be aborted temporarily due to suspicion as a result of his historic role as a persecutor of Christians. Galatians 2:1-10 and Acts 21:17-25 would suggest that a healthy relationship was secured as a consequence of this initial meeting. See Nicholas Taylor, *Paul, Antioch, and Jerusalem: A Study in Relationships and Authority in Earliest Christianity*, Journal for the Study of the New Testament 66 (Sheffield: JSOT Press, 1992), 75–83.

[41] Stephen D. Renn, ed., *Expository Dictionary of Bible Words: Word Studies for Key English Bible Words Based on the Hebrew and Greek Texts* (Peabody: Hendrickson Publishers, 2005), 536.

baptism (by a particular church) is always into 'membership' of the one universal church, never into a specific local church.[42] 'Baptism is the initiating oath-sign of the new covenant. God means for his new covenant people to be visible, and one enters that people through baptism.'[43] Furthermore, 'The new covenant is more than an invisible, spiritual reality. It has a visible, public shape, and baptism draws the edges of that shape...since the new covenant creates a public people, entrance into the covenant requires a public promise, namely baptism.'[44] This principle is repeated consistently throughout Acts (e.g. Acts 8:12, 38, 9:18, 10:47-48, 16:14-15, 31-33, 18:8 19:5).

When boiled down to its barest essence, liberating us from focussing only on Baptistic ecclesiology, Leeman argues membership within the local church of any form is a list of names affirmed by the apostolic church for the sake of giving witness to Christ. It is this list, written, verbal or otherwise, which the church must maintain an interest in overseeing, disciplining and equipping toward greater Christlikeness.[45] Such a mandate requires leadership.

The Acts narrative, presuming leadership development rather than explaining it, chronicles the emergence of new churches and leaders (Apostles, Elders, Deacons) who shaped and led designated groups through tribulation (e.g. Ac.4:1–22, 5:17–42, 7:54–8:3, 13:44–52, 14:19, 16:16–24, 17:5–9, 13, 19:23–41, 20:28). These leaders were charged

---

[42] Michael Root and Risto Saarinen, eds., *Baptism and the Unity of the Church* (Grand Rapids: W.B. Eerdmans, 1998), 15–16.
[43] Bobby Jamieson, *Going Public: Why Baptism Is Required for Church Membership* (Nashville: B&H Publishing Group, 2015), 19. The new covenant will be considered further in chapter 4.
[44] Bobby Jamieson, Going Public, 77.
[45] Leeman, *The Church and the Surprising Offense of God's Love*, 292.

with overseeing the church within the context of a mutually accountable relationship which sometimes required the exercising of discipline (e.g. 1 Cor. 5:4-5; Rom.16:17; 2 Thess.3:6-15; Phil.3:17-19). However, Scripture is silent regarding a prescribed ecclesiological structure through which this should be achieved (other than being defined as 'punishment inflicted by the majority,' 2 Cor.2:6). Discipline mostly required avoidance (e.g. Rom.16:17; 2 Thess.3:6; 2 Tim.3:5; Tit.3:5, 3:10) but, on occasions, necessitated removal from the church (e.g. 1 Cor.5:2,13).

Arguably, the application of publicly corroborated discipline (cf. 1 Cor.5:4; 2 Cor.2:6-8) could be implemented only if the individuals concerned had entered into a mutually covenanted relationship with a visible church, as their localised expression of being part of the invisible church. Covenant relationship, regardless of how formalised, seems likely; otherwise, churches and their leaders would have been reliant upon the goodwill of those being disciplined to absent themselves for the good of the wider fellowship. Based upon personal experience, such acquiescence is the exception, not the rule. Leeman argues that 'Christ does not call us to join a church, but to submit to a church;'[46] such submission requires some level of agreement if sanctions have any validity. Allied to this line of thinking, Scripture defines leadership responsibilities and submission to that leadership, which, again, requires mutual accountability locally, not trans-locally, and certainly not universally (e.g. Heb.13:17).

When the church at Antioch is born after the martyrdom of Stephen (Ac.11:19-30), despite itinerant leadership from

---

[46] Jonathan Leeman, *The Church and the Surprising Offense of God's Love,* 30.

Jerusalem, there is still no indication given yet of how the church was structured. There is evidence however of the inter-dependence of distinct, geographically disparate, groupings of believers through the sending of aid (e.g. Ac.11:29-30).

From Acts 13 onwards, when some of the prophets and teachers in Antioch were worshipping and fasting, the Spirit set apart Barnabas and Saul for a particular work. They did not send the whole church or even the whole leadership team, but a representative delegation (Ac.13:1-3). The decision-making process seems unceremonious humanly speaking, but by this time 'church' had come, synonymously and without well-defined distinction, to represent Christians universally *and* a local body of believers, including small groups.[47] The universal (invisible) church and the local (visible) church are therefore not mutually exclusive. The implication, supported by other references in Scripture (e.g. 1 Thess.1:1; Eph.4:1-3), is that we are to be connected to a specific visible church in a particular context, by agreement (Ac.9:26-28), as a microcosmic expression of our organic 'membership' of the invisible church through faith in Christ (Rom.12:4-5; 1 Cor.12:27). 'The institutional space the kingdom of heaven occupies on earth *is* the local church.'[48]

As the narration of the early church continues, the sense of belonging to a specific church, under the leadership of appointed leaders, persists. For example, Paul and Barnabas appointed Elders before leaving them to lead the church in their absence (Ac.14:22-23). While we do not know how the church was structured or who was leading

---

[47] Ward, *Liquid Church.*, 98.
[48] Bobby Jamieson, *Going Public*, 82.

the church before Paul and Barnabas returned, it seems the believers were meeting together in an undisclosed, unstructured, but not unordered, way (e.g. Ac.15:22). Specifically, natural leaders may have been functioning from each church's inception, but only recognised officially retrospectively. It stands to reason, therefore, that there must have been a definite group of people who believed foremost and then 'belonged' to each church. This idea is further consolidated when Paul and Barnabas leave Antioch (Ac.15:2-4, 22-23, 16:4); they were welcomed and commissioned by the whole church, albeit there is no indication of a 'membership' structure or of whom 'the whole church' consisted.

From the example of the church in Acts, we can conclude that while 'Membership' is not a concept unambiguously found in Scripture, principles we might associate with membership (i.e. regenerate faith, belonging, commitment, being a worshipper, mutual accountability, engaged in mission and ministry through gift sharing) are identifiable and find systematic theological maturation.

The words 'member' and 'members' are used in and through Paul's repeated and variously applied 'Body of Christ' metaphor (Ro.12:4-8; 1 Cor.12:12-31; Eph.5:25-30; Col.2:19) but this anatomical metaphor is not, per se, speaking about membership so much as it is about the essential, non-individualistic, nature of belonging and remaining accountable to Christ the 'head.' Morris argues the Body metaphor, which we shall return to in chapter 4, was commonly used by ancient writers to depict the State, but Paul appropriates the image to emphasise the church's gift-giving unity with diversity while challenging homogeneity.[49] Leeman reasons Paul uses this metaphor in a confused ambiguity, simultaneously incorporating local and universal applications of church belonging since, as argued above, the universal is present in the local,[50] thus reminding believers of their obligation to submit to Christ under the authority invested in the local church and its overseers, notwithstanding mutual peer-to-peer accountability.[51]

In short, faith in Christ creates a permanent, not prosthetic, attachment to the Body; therefore, commitment to that Body is not an optional extra for the Christian. Morris helpfully summarises that there is 'a relational reality' underpinning all the different images used within the New Testament (e.g. Ac.20:28; 2 Cor.6:18; Eph.2:19; 1 Pe.2:5; Rev.19:7-8, 21:9) to depict the church, which is especially true of the Body of Christ metaphor.[52] The relational aspect of belonging to the church universal and local should not, therefore, be overlooked.[53] As Leeman argues and as I will further discuss in chapter 5, we do not attend a family meal simply because there is good food on offer, we do so by consequence of our privileged familial association.[54]

Historical Basis For Baptist Membership

Readers from other denominational groupings will need learn their own history to make sound application, but, for

---

[49] Helen Morris, *Flexible Church*, 65–66.
[50] Jonathan Leeman, *The Church and the Surprising Offense of God's Love*, 209.
[51] Jonathan Leeman, *The Church and the Surprising Offence of God's Love*, 208–13.
[52] Helen Morris, *Flexible Church,* 67–68.
[53] The relational aspect of Membership will be considered further in Chapter 4.
[54] Jonathan Leeman, *The Church and the Surprising Offense of God's Love*, 136. This concept is foundational to the conclusions drawn in Chapter 5, which lead to the possibility of understanding and expressing Baptist ecclesiology differently from Restaurant Ecclesiology.

now, I share the history of my own denomination to highlight how history informs present ecclesiology.

Baptist ecclesiology has its origins in nonconformity and mercurial martyrdom. In the Reformation period of the early 16th century, Sattler, a leading Anabaptist,[55] controversially produced the Schleitheim Confession.[56] This declaration of faith, a theological counteraction against Catholicism, rejected by the established Catholic Church amongst other theological controversies, stated that 'infant baptism was an abomination from the Pope and Christian baptism came following repentance and faith only.' Subsequent doctrinal enmity caused the killing of more Anabaptists in the 16th century than all the martyrs of the early church preceding them.[57] Consequently, association with this fresh expression of church, particularly through formalised membership, like in the early church, was circumspectly considered by candidates.

Despite persecution, early Baptists considered they had ascertained the blueprint for a Biblical ecclesiology: 'For this, the Baptists bore cheerfully, cruel mockings, and scourgings; yea, moreover bonds and imprisonments, and death.'[58] Given this background, a robust baptistic ecclesiology developed headlining the contention that the

---

[55] The Anabaptists were a diverse and radical movement at the time of The Reformation, who are generally seen to be an offshoot of Protestantism (albeit some Anabaptists dispute this). The core facets of Anabaptist theology are baptism for adult believers only; the symbolism of Holy Communion for baptised believers only; religious separation (including the separation of church and state); non-resistance. See William Roscoe Estep, *The Anabaptist Story: An Introduction to Sixteenth-Century Anabaptism* (Grand Rapids: William B. Eerdmans Pub, 1996), 9-28.
[56] Michael Sattler, translated by J.C.Wenger, 'The Schleitheim Confession of Faith' in *The Mennonite Quarterly Review*, XIX, 4 (October 1945), 247-253.
[57] Grace Davie, *Religion in Britain since 1945*, 1–9.
[58] Edward Bean Underhill, *Records Of A Church of Christ*, xliv.

true church is a congregation of 'visible saints.'[59] Thus, their faith was not clandestine. Those who did not exhibit visible signs in their lifestyles (e.g. an outward profession of faith, baptism, practical enjoyment of the sacraments, sound morality, etc.) would be disregarded from this company of visible saints. In the words of the 1644 First London Confession of Faith, the local church is 'a company of visible saints, called and separated from the world, by the word and Spirit of God, to the visible profession of the faith of the Gospel being baptised into that faith, and joined to the Lord and each other by mutual agreement.'[60]

Baptists defined their Membership commitment as publicly 'giving yourself up to the Lord [vertically] and to the church [horizontally] to watch over and to be watched over'[61] which succinctly captures the desire for membership to be a two-dimensional, cruciform, mutually accountable covenant, rather than a desultory enrolment within a social or jurisdictive institution. Paul similarly exhorts a cruciform commitment: 'First, they gave themselves [vertically] to the Lord; and then, by God's will, they gave themselves [horizontally] to us as well' (2 Cor.8:5).

The early Baptists adopted many elements of broader Anabaptist doctrine, and from this confession sprang the discipline determining how believers should live and worship together,[62] discriminatorily filtering admittance into their church on the precondition that faith preceded

---

[59] Michael A.G.Haykin, 'The Baptist Identity: A View From the Eighteenth Century', *The Evangelical Quarterly*, EQ67:2 (1995), 137-152.
[60] The First London Baptist Confession of Faith 33 reproduced in Lumpkin and Leonard, *Baptist Confessions of Faith*, 165.
[61] Nigel Wright, *Challenge to Change*. (Kingsway, 1991), 112.
[62] Geoffrey G Reynolds and Berkshire Baptist Association, *First among Equals*. (Oxford: 1993), 53.

History Informing The Present 31

baptism. Underlying this restriction was the conviction that 'religion is a matter of private conscience rather than public order; that the church is a fellowship of believers rather than an army of pressed men [and women].'[63] Accordingly, membership was not primarily about assent to Christian doctrine, but about commitment to a particular way of evidencing their 'visible' regenerate faith and discipleship.[64] Members' Meetings were concerned primarily with discipleship and exercising disciplinary sanctions over any who disappointed, more than they were about managing the 'business' of the church.

As already elucidated, joining such a community in the 16th century was a life and death decision concerning the law which philosophically assumed that everybody was part of the State church. Membership entrusted a person into a covenant, where a solemn agreement was entered into between believers [horizontally], before and for the glory of God [vertically]. As the church grew, new assemblies adopted similar models of covenant alongside a confession of faith. Similarly, churches fellowshipping together, in the same way as individuals, arguably representing an early form of union membership which, not without theological contention over various controversial issues, still exists today in the form of the Baptist Union.[65] Confessions dealt with what one believed; covenants mutually concurred how one would subsequently live. These early covenants between individuals were based upon a mutual bond of love, together with willing accountability to watch over

---

[63] B. R. White, 'The Doctrine of the Church in the Particular Baptist Confession of 1644', *The Journal of Theological Studies*, N.S., 19 (1968), 580, 582, 590; Michael R. Watts, *The Dissenters* (Oxford, 1978), 34.

[64] B. R. White, *'The English Baptists of the Seventeenth Century,' A History of the English Baptists*, v. 1 (London: Baptist Historical Society, 1983), 22.

[65] Geoffrey G. Reynolds and Berkshire Baptist Association, *First among Equals*, 108.

each other morally, doctrinally and prayerfully. They called this 'walking together' which provided a comforting sense of identity for those who had absconded from the national church.[66]

Seeking to emphasise the mutually enduring explorational, pioneering and prophetic nature of such a relationship, Payne more latterly expanded the 'walking together' apophthegm to include 'in ways known and to be made known.'[67] Fundamentally, responsibility for guaranteeing the covenant between God and his people, and that which bound his people together, was entrusted to all the people of God, not exclusively to ecclesiastical or political elites.[68] This practice evolved, requiring those wanting to join the church to sign the covenant as a public pledge according to the established standards and expectations of the congregation. 'The drawing up of a covenant and the committing of it to writing added to its solemnity; the appending of the signatures...both underlined its binding character and satisfied their self-consciousness as individuals.'[69]

These historical roots have substantively shaped the development and practices of contemporary Baptist churches.[70] Aside from nuanced differences, churches, at

---

[66] Paul Fiddes in B. R. White et al., eds., *Pilgrim Pathways: Essays in Baptist History in Honour of B.R. White* (Macon: Mercer University Press, 1999), 50.
[67] E.A.Payne, *Ways Known And To Be Made Known* (London: Baptist Union of Great Britain and Ireland, 1977).
[68] Paul Fiddes in B. R. White et al., eds., *Pilgrim Pathways: Essays in Baptist History in Honour of B.R. White* (Macon: Mercer University Press, 1999), 47–74.
[69] Geoffrey F Nuttall, *Visible Saints: The Congregational Way, 1640-1660* (Oxford: Basil Blackwell, 1957), 78.
[70] Space does not allow for a full discussion of Baptist history since these foundational beginnings. For a full and detailed narration, see White et al., *Pilgrim Pathways*, 1999.

least theoretically, continue to organise around similar principles affirming enduring regenerate commitment to Christ [vertically] and, significantly, to members of the local church [horizontally]. While some churches have constitutionally lessened the requirement for baptism, nonetheless, and again I stress theoretically, becoming a member of a Baptist church continues to demand a non-elective sacrificial participatory commitment to God *and* fellow believers (albeit without fear of persecution).

Pagitt perfectly expresses the idealistic understanding of such participation: 'Community is where real spiritual formation happens...community as a means of spiritual formation serves to immerse people in the Christian way of living so that they learn how to be Christian in a life-long process of discovery and change. The Christian community can and should be a context for evangelism and discipleship, a place where faith is professed and lived.'[71] Chester and Timms similarly argue that 'Our identity as human beings is found in community. Our identity as Christians is found in Christ's new community.'[72]

Contemporary Expectations of Church Membership

As the review of history above accentuates, Baptist ecclesiology is fuelled by the conviction that the church should have obvious demarcations. This will be similarly true of other denominational and non-denominational contexts.

Bray argues, 'the church, whatever else it may be, is still at

---

[71] Doug Pagitt, *Church Re-Imagined: The Spiritual Formation of People in Communities of Faith* (Grand Rapids: Youth Specialties, 2005), 27.
[72] Tim Chester and Steve Timmis, *Total Church: A Radical Reshaping around Gospel and Community* (Nottingham: Inter-Varsity Press, 2010), 50.

heart the community of those who have been born of the Spirit of God.'[73] Starkly stated, 'inside' should be those who have a regenerate faith and 'outside' should remain those who have not. Leeman affirms that this defined boundary has biblical precedent (e.g. 1 Cor.5:12-13; Gal.6:10) but recognises such delineation can become an exclusive impediment, making 'insiders' and 'outsiders' alike feel judgementally nervous.[74]

Anthropologist, Hiebert, articulates my felt reality locally: such a potentially selective approach, even if biblical, classifies people according to static conceptions of what they are, demanding that someone within the institutional hierarchy must act as arbiter of any given individual's testimony. Consequently, Hiebert contends, 'the church focuses all its attention on patrolling the boundaries, making sure the right people are on the 'inside' and the wrong people are on the 'outside.''[75]

Binary conceptions are entirely appropriate regarding the salvific foundations for anyone claiming to be a Christian, but such dogmatic classifications become subjectively problematic long-term because they do not allow for the seasonal and subtle ebb and flow of a person's faith in Christ [vertically] *or* their fluctuating commitment to the church [horizontally]. There is a dynamic, non-binary, complexity of factors which, despite best intentions, cause faith and commitment to seasonally diminish or flourish.

Volf argues that 'the boundary between those who belong

---

[73] Gerald Lewis Bray, *The Church: A Theological and Historical Account* (Grand Rapids: Baker Academic, 2016), 216.
[74] Jonathan Leeman, *The Church and the Surprising Offense of God's Love*, 164.
[75] Paul G. Hiebert, *Anthropological Reflections on Missiological Issues* (Grand Rapids: Baker Books, 1994), 115–16.

to the church and those who do not, should not be drawn too sharply...the establishment of clear boundaries is usually an act of violence.'[76] To some extent, I concur. Membership is a dichotomy between love (including grace) and structure (incorporating Truth, rules, resources, hierarchies), serving and submission. At its worst, membership can be perceived as an exclusivist boundary between the saved and unsaved, committed and uncommitted, the wholehearted and the half-hearted. This perception is unfortunate, albeit not unprecedented: 'Communities of all kinds establish boundaries, to include some and exclude others. Churches are no different.'[77]

Writing on the theme of deinstitutionalisation, Morris argues that church communities should be dialogical, not monological, albeit forms of institutionalisation[78] are essential, even inevitable, to nurture depth of relationship and commitment since relationships do not flourish through informality alone.[79] On this point, I agree, however, she further contends, supported by various other theologians including Turner, Healy, Lincoln and Arnold, that 'Paul could not conceive of a church with no structure

---

[76] Miroslav Volf, *After Our Likeness: The Church as the Image of the Trinity*, Sacra Doctrina (Grand Rapids: William B. Eerdmans, 1998), 151.

[77] Stuart Murray, *Church Planting: Laying Foundations*, North American ed (Scottdale, Pa: Herald Press, 2001), 180.

[78] Derivatives of the word 'institution' are used neutrally in this book unless otherwise stated. Some contemporary thinkers might have negative perceptions of institutions. Huntington's definition helps convey such neutrality: Institutions are 'stable, valued, recurring patterns of behaviour.' See Samuel P. Huntington and Francis Fukuyama, *Political Order in Changing Societies* (New Haven: Yale Univ. Press, 2006), 12.

[79] Helen Morris, *Flexible Church*, 103–13.

or order.'[80] 'An absence of structure is, in practice, a lack of commitment on the part of individuals to any routinised engagement with God [vertically] and others [horizontally].'[81] I disagree, contending that there is a significant distinction to be made between 'structure' and 'order.'

Paul says little about ecclesiological 'structure' and even less about institutionalised engagement with God; he does, however, have much to say regarding beneficial ecclesiological 'order' (e.g. 1 Cor.14:26-40; Eph.4:11-16; Tit.1:5; Ro.12:4-8; 1 Tim.3:1-16). Therefore, we should 'pause when trying to use the New Testament as a model for our common life today...it is impossible, on the basis of what we know, to build a complete church structure out of the evidence of what we have.'[82] Consequently, if structure is a dialogical ecclesiological necessity for good order, (which I think it is), it is for pragmatic reasoning more than theological or doctrinal compulsion.

Although a 'membership roll' is not indispensable theologically, a list which is associated to some form of covenant is necessary, for, at the very least, pragmatic reasons, to manage ministry and discipline regardless, as a viable and visible expression of the invisible church. That said, if membership expresses nothing more than a name

---

[80] Helen Morris, *Flexible Church*, 110. referencing Nicholas M. Healy, *Church, World, and the Christian Life: Practical-Prophetic Ecclesiology*, Cambridge Studies in Christian Doctrine (Cambridge: Cambridge University Press, 2000), 589–601; Andrew T. Lincoln et al., *Ephesians*, Nachdr., Word Biblical Commentary, [General ed.: David A. Hubbard; Glenn W. Barker. Old Testament ed.: John D. W. Watts. New Testament ed.: Ralph P. Martin]; Vol. 42 (Waco: Word Books, 2005), 229–33; Clinton E Arnold, *Power and Magic: The Concept of Power in Ephesians* (Cambridge: Cambridge University Press, 1989), 159.
[81] Helen Morris, *Flexible Church*, 112.
[82] Gerald Lewis Bray, *The Church*, 50.

on a database, such commitment is of little significance beyond the expectation of financial contributions and the reciprocal right to vote in congregational meetings to mechanically rubberstamp decisions already presupposed at a leadership level. Regrettably, the experience of many local churches does, albeit episodically and unintentionally, stumble into this mentality. Understandably, some might interpret this as coercive leadership and lip-service to authentic Christocratic forms of governance. At its best, however, membership can be one of the most fulfilling aspects of a person's Christian walk as together, in unity and diversity, we discern the heart of Christ.

In summary, we can conclude the following: there is no discussion of membership as such in the New Testament, but particular conditions for 'membership' by way of belonging and commitment are implied in the metaphors used. Paul compares the members of the church to organic parts of a body, reminding them of their indispensable gift-sharing function in the universal body into which they were baptised as expressed locally. Multifariously, the New Testament indicates that membership/belonging benefits for those 'inside' may cease for reasons of discipline (1 Cor.5:12-13; Tit.2:15; 2 Thes.3:14; Matt.18:15-17).

Although the evidence for formalised Membership in the New Testament is implicit, the principles for belonging to a local church are consistent and have enduringly been so in my Baptist tradition. Leeman's view of Membership provides a helpful concluding statement: 'Church membership...gives structure or shape to what it means to be a Christian – a person who displays God's love;'[83] I would add '...and love of God and the household of believers.'

---

[83] Jonathan Leeman, *The Church and the Surprising Offence of God's Love*, 19.

3 | Socio-Psychological Explorations

In chapter 1, the problem of Restaurant Ecclesiology was described, highlighting symptoms which, viewed through the lens of a stereotypical and macro snapshot, reveal an incongruence between the commitment of the SAGA-generation and the pre-SAGA generations.

In chapter 2, historical and biblical perspectives relating to this contemporary problem were explored, underlining historic biblical and a particularly baptistic emphasis regarding the Christocratic, cruciform, relational nature of ecclesiology.

In this chapter, consideration will be given to the socio-psychological factors contributing to Restaurant Ecclesiology. Such a study is essential since the practice of faith is contextual and subsequently never immune from the influence of dominant societal factors. These influences will be considered by exploring sociological and psychological theory as autonomous disciplines, recognising however that there is overlap between these two disciplines.

Sociological Factors

Sociology is primarily concerned with how societal forces socialise and shape behaviour.[84] Arguably, the most influential sociological shift impacting Restaurant Ecclesiology is the transition from modernity into postmodernity which is where I shall begin.[85]

Postmodernity vs The Modern Era

Sweet starkly contrasts these two paradigms: 'If the Modern Era was a rage for order, regulation, stability, singularity, and fixity, the Postmodern Era is a rage for chaos, uncertainty, otherness, openness, multiplicity and change.'[86] More concisely, postmodernity is a mode of observing and then engaging with the world in such a way that ridged conceptions of existence are perpetually distrusted.

Postmodernism gained ascendency in the mid-late 20th century through the work of Foucault;[87] it promotes scepticism and the rejection of historically embraced meta-narratives, especially those which are socially conditioned

---

[84] Jeffrey C Alexander and Kenneth Thompson, *A Contemporary Introduction to Sociology: Culture and Society in Transition* (Boulder: Paradigm Publishers, 2008), 2–29.

[85] A variety of scholars argue that postmodernism is an exaggeration of modernity, better labelled as late-modernity and that the reality of its effects has been exaggerated; contemporary experience, therefore, is just another phase of modernity. See José López, ed., *After Postmodernism: An Introduction to Critical Realism*, Reprinted, Continuum Studies in Critical Theory (London: Athlone Press, 2006), 4; Alan Kirby, "The death of postmodernism and beyond." *Philosophy Now*, 58 (2006); Marc Cools ed et al, *Safety, Societal Problems and Citizen's Perceptions: New Empirical Data, Theories and Analyses*, Governance of Security Research Paper Series (Antwerpen: Maklu, 2010), 88.

[86] Leonard I. Sweet, *AquaChurch 2.0: Piloting Your Church in Today's Fluid Culture* (Colorado Springs: David C Cook, 2008), 24.

[87] Lewis Call, *Postmodern Anarchism* (Lanham: Lexington Books, 2002), 65.

assumptions of the Enlightenment period.[88] Postmodernity is a reaction against scientific attempts to explain reality, particularly those conflicting with or inconsiderate of personal circumstance.[89] Postmodernism advances a life philosophy which confronts the ideological, social, institutional and historical structures that seek to shape contemporary culture.[90]

According to sociologist Giddens, who argues postmodernity is a radicalised and hyper-technological continuation of latter forms of modernity,[91] postmodernity is ideologically characterised by the world being open to transformation through human intervention; a complex of economic institutions, especially industrial production and a market economy; a specific range of political institutions, including the nation-state and mass democracy.[92] Bauman, like Giddens, is against using the 'postmodernity' descriptor, preferring to characterise contemporary sociological symptoms as a transitional continuity from solid modernity to more liquid forms of social life, 'liquid modernity.'[93] Bauman contends that within this worldview, a person can shift their opinion from one social position to another fluidly, thus freeing themselves from imposed historical restrictions. The archetypal features of modernity are secularisation, scientific rationalism, ordered

---

[88] Andreas Huyssen, *After the Great Divide: Modernism, Mass Culture, Postmodernism* (New York: ACLS Humanities E-Book), 188.

[89] Basit Bilal Koshul, *The Postmodern Significance of Max Weber's Legacy: Disenchanting Disenchantment* (New York: Palgrave Macmillan, 2005), 46–47.

[90] Douglas Kellner, *Media Culture: Cultural Studies, Identity, and Politics between the Modern and the Postmodern* (London: Routledge, 1995).

[91] Richard Appignanesi et al., *Introducing Postmodernism* (New York: Totem Books, 1995), 126.

[92] Richard Appignanesi et al., *Introducing Postmodernism*, 126.

[93] Zygmunt Bauman, *Liquid Modernity* (Cambridge: Polity Press, 2000), 1-15.

institutions and clear social structure (e.g. class, gender and family) which, in turn, influence the individual. In contrast, the foremost features of postmodernism are individualisation and its interrelated symptoms: consumerism, commitment phobia and anti-authoritarianism; and globalisation.[94]

Regardless of the academic debate surrounding the label, theorists constructively highlight that there is divergence in the way differing generations view the world. As such, I will employ the critical features of postmodernism listed above to differentiate between the worldviews of the SAGA and pre-SAGA generation(s) since, stereotypically,[95] the SAGA generation are modernists, and the pre-SAGA generation(s) are postmodernists, or, more accurately, are typical of Bauman's 'liquid moderns' who vacillate between the two typologies with considerable fluidity.[96] In his critique of these sociological definitions, James, using less bounded labels, insightfully comments that all sociological shifts are constructs of 'overlaying and overlapping' processes which

---

[94] Marshall Berman, *All That Is Solid Melts into Air*, 15–36.

[95] The SAGA and pre-SAGA classifications are generalist stereotypes. On occasions, the SAGA generation also reflect some or all of postmodernisms values fluidly. Perhaps this is to be expected, as previously argued, these 'baby-boomers' were the forerunners of anti-authority, individualism and globalisation in the 1960s. Scepticism was very much promoted. Some argue that this generation was more anti-establishment and more rebellious than the 'Thatcherite' and the consumerist generation that followed. See Ben Agger, *A Critical Theory Of Public Life: Knowledge, Discourse And Politics In An Age Of Decline*. (Hoboken: Taylor and Francis, 2013), 199–202. Bruce Cannon Gibney, *A Generation of Sociopaths: How the Baby Boomers Betrayed America* (New York: Hachette Books, 2017). Both these sociologists argue that modernists, despite blaming postmoderns, live in a state of projected denial regarding the negative influence they had upon societal values.

[96] It should be noted that there are many variables within these generalisations which might include parenting styles, individualistic/community minded cultures, religious beliefs (Christian or other), wealth, societal structure and cultural practice.

do not necessarily replace what has gone before.[97]

In understanding one's ecclesiology, James' thesis is insightful since, as argued in chapter 2, ecclesiological development is an 'overlaying and overlapping' of doctrine, theology and tradition which has continuity with the past, further influenced by sociological and contextual phenomena. Such overlapping and overlaying will be evident within the differing perspectives of any cross-generational congregation who bestride overgeneralised binary modernity/postmodernity classifications, causing most local churches to be more 'plasmatic' than liquid or solid. For example, in my local church, some of our SAGA generation, influenced and transformed as their social context, are more fluidly modern than the so-called 'liquid moderns' who can likewise be unconventionally ridged if contextually stimulated. That said, the archetypal features of postmodernity, individualism (alongside its derivatives: consumerism, commitment phobia, anti-authoritarianism) and globalisation, will now be considered with regard to commitment.

Individualisation

Individualisation is a structural characteristic of highly differentiated societies which perpetuates an ambivalence towards altruism and sacrificial investment into social capita.[98] Taylor argues that hedonism and consumerism (see below) have conspired together, resulting in a self-centred individualistic pursuit to find, realise and release

---

[97] Paul James in *Making Modernity from the Mashriq to the Maghreb*, "They Have Never Been Modern? Then What Is the Problem with Those Persians?" 31–54. (Melbourne: Arena Publications, 2015), 31-54.

[98] Ulrich Beck and Elisabeth Beck-Gernsheim, *Individualization: Institutionalized Individualism and Its Social and Political Consequences*, Theory, Culture & Society (London: SAGE, 2002), 1–21.

oneself.[99] The majority of voluntary organisations are impacted by individualism, collectively struggling to recruit and retain volunteers, members and leaders from the pre-SAGA generation(s).[100] Various social factors contribute to this reality, most notably greater complexity and pressure around work/life balance, alongside ever-increasing emphasis upon the importance of personal liberty, resulting in more temporary, transient lifestyles which offer negligible long-term security.

This insecurity is further compounded by augmented social mobility resulting in the geographic dispersion of and consequent relational isolation from extended (frequently fragmented) families. Moreover, adults are choosing to 'settle down' later in life than in previous generations, precipitating in first-time parents being comparatively older, and thus having less residual time and financial capacity than their predecessors at the corresponding life stage.

The pre-SAGA generations are, or at least have the perception they are, time and/or resource poor.[101] Putman's research reveals that this contributes to a decrease in civic engagement and diminished investment into social capita compared to the modern era.[102] A protracted downward trajectory has continued since

---

[99] Charles Taylor, *A Secular Age* (Harvard University Press, 2007), 18–19, 473–89.
[100] Anne Wollenberg, *'Image Problem Turn Recruits Away,'* The Guardian, citing the UK 2007-2008 Citizenship Survey, accessed July 15, 2019, https://www.theguardian.com/society/2008/sep/10/voluntarysector.volunteering
[101] Ulrich Beck and Elisabeth Beck-Gernsheim, *Individualization, 42-53*.
[102] Robert D. Putnam, *Bowling Alone: The Collapse and Revival of American Community* (New York: Simon & Schuster, 2001), 93-115.

Putman's research, only now starting to plateau.[103]

Ironically, a challenging consequence of an individualist mindset is that employers increasingly offer opportunities to 'volunteer' in the Third Sector as contractual obligations and/or employment benefits. Remunerated-volunteerism 'make[s] them [employees] feel like there is a larger purpose to their lives than just meeting financial goals...this need is only getting stronger with the younger generation, the Postmoderns.'[104] Such employment 'benefits' are accompanied by requirements for higher productivity, increased efficiency and intensified, potentially excessive, effort from employees.[105]

The postmodernists' situation is exacerbated by the pervasion of electronic communication streams beyond the conventional workplace. In contrast, the SAGA-generation achieved such charitable philanthropy without employer intervention, with weightier support from extended family, and, significantly, without extra-curricular electronic impositions. Individualisation, as a reaction against the regulated world, is the root cause of consumerism, commitment phobia and anti-authoritarianism which, Moynagh contends, 'represents a profound ethical turn: the expressive rather than dutiful self dominates society –

---

[103] UK Civil Society Almnac 2019, *'How Many People Volunteer and What Do They Do'* accessed July 15, 2019, https://data.ncvo.org.uk/volunteering/

[104] Karl Moore and Richard Pound, cited in Helen Morris, *Flexible Church: Being the Church in the Contemporary World.* (London: SCM Press, 2019), 35.

[105] Francis Green, Alan Felstead, Duncan Gallie and Golo Henseke, *'Work Intensity in Britain: First Findings from the Skills and Employment Survey 2017'* (Cardiff: Cardiff University, 2017) accessed June 25, 2019, https://www.cardiff.ac.uk/__data/assets/pdf_file/0009/1309455/4_Intensity_Minireport_Final.pdf

and increasingly the church.'[106]

Consumerism

Sociologist, Davie, emphasises that consumerism is a significant culture shift, affecting all institutions, especially the Church. She describes a shift from orthodox 'modernist obligation' to non-orthodox 'postmodernist consumption,' arguing that the centre of gravity of the lived faith moves from collective patterns towards an individual pilgrimage.[107] Berger and Zijderveld state that the same is true for the acceptance of doctrines or moral prescriptions, contending that the consumerist age is a *'bricolage'* where one composes a bespoke package of beliefs to suit personal circumstance.[108]

Postmodernism thus promotes scepticism toward the anchorage of doctrine or dogma where orthodoxy (right belief) is being substituted with orthopraxy (right practice) which is primarily determined by pragmatic philosophical considerations popularised by the majority voice.[109] Clark asserts that consumerism risks divorcing belief from practice, creating a 'perverted liturgy' leading to a misplaced, misdirected focus[110] and, I would add, a misshapen and ephemeral ecclesiology driven by dissatisfying expediency and pragmatism. Subsequently,

---

[106] Michael Moynagh and Philip Harrold, *Church for Every Context: An Introduction to Theology and Practice* (London: SCM Press, 2012), 83.

[107] Grace Davie, *The Sociology of Religion: A Critical Agenda*, Second edition (Los Angeles: SAGE, 2013), 96.

[108] Peter Berger and Anton Zijderveld, *In Praise of Doubt: How to Have Convictions Without Becoming a Fanatic* (New York: HarperOne, 2014), 25–48.

[109] David Trementozzi and Amos Yong, *Salvation in the Flesh: Understanding How Embodiment Shapes Christian Faith* (Eugene: McMaster Divinity College Press, 2018), 109–56.

[110] Jason Clarke in Helen Morris, *Flexible Church: Being the Church in the Contemporary World*. (London: SCM Press, 2019), 35.

argues Sayers, 'Post-Christian culture attempts to attain the solace of faith, whilst gutting it of the costs, commitments and restraints that the gospel places on the individual will...Post-Christianity is Christianity emptied of its content.'[111]

Lyon argues that while religion is not declining under postmodernity's influence, it is relocating to 'the sphere of consumption' with the growth of consumer culture as people selectively choose how and when to engage.[112] Consumerism has unambiguous resonance with Restaurant Ecclesiology where 'members weigh up their options before promising to attend the next meeting, and that promise is broken if a better offer comes along. The individual reigns supreme.'[113]

The logical conclusion of an identity rooted in consumerism is an expectation to have ones needs perpetually satisfied. The historic biblical explorations in Chapter 2 would suggest that authentic, countercultural Christianity, however, ought to be instituted upon more than what Moynagh calls 'a transactional approach.'[114] Should membership of the church be characterised by obligated household service, not marketplace consumption? Further critique of this question will be explored in the chapters which follow.

---

[111] Mark Sayers, Disappearing Church: From Cultural Relevance to Gospel Resilience, (Chicago: Moody Publishers, 2016), 17

[112] David Lyon, *Jesus in Disneyland: Religion in Postmodern Times* (Cambridge: Polity Press, 2000), 73-96.

[113] Eddie Gibbs and Ian Coffey, *Church Next: Quantum Changes in How We Do Ministry* (Leicester: Inter-Varsity Press, 2001), 225.

[114] Michael Moynagh, *Changing World, Changing Church: New Forms of Church, out-of-the-Pew Thinking, Initiatives That Work* (London: Monarch Books, 2003), 31.

Commitment Phobia

Schwarz argues that individualist consumers swim in a sea of choice, creating a paradox: more choice diminishes the attractiveness of what could be chosen, resulting in lessened commitment to that which is ultimately selected.[115] Furthermore, pressure on available time and resource propagates a reluctance to invest because such commitment invariably incorporates the burden of associated responsibilities. Consequently, requests for greater commitment within the church (i.e. meetings, committees, home groups, outreach programs, etc.) are no longer perceived as covenant commitment characteristics, as they might have been historically, but rather as embezzlement of the scarce resource of personal/family liberty.[116] The consequential outcome is 'commitment phobia,' a phrase which used to be reserved for insecure pre-marital couples, but now can be applied to relationships with institutional bodies.

Colson and Larson argue that 'a Christian without commitment is an oxymoron.'[117] Personal experience asserts that people are not commitment-phobic because they are unsympathetic or unsupportive of our values and vision, but such phobia significantly redefines the extent to which they will participate. For example, as previously stated, regenerate believers are happy to become members, confirming synergy with the vision and values of any local church, but the outworking of that diverges

---

[115] Barry Schwartz, *The Paradox of Choice: Why More Is Less* (New York: Harper Perennial, 2007), 9-22.
[116] The theme of covenant commitment will be further considered in chapter 4.
[117] Chuck Colson and Catherine Larson, 'The Lost Art Of Commitment', *Christianity Today*, 04 August 2010,
https://www.christianitytoday.com/ct/2010/august/10.49.html.

between the differing generations.

Enigmatically, organisations which are reporting an increase in membership (e.g. The National Trust,[118] gyms,[119] etc.), despite the decline in other spheres, do not demand mutually binding relational commitments from their members, aside from their financial subscription and enjoying the benefits at their discretion. This is a different understanding of 'membership' to the cruciform commitment described in Chapter 2, presuming zero decision-making engagement in the organisational hierarchy and negligible accountability with other members. Although to a lesser extent, Restaurant Ecclesiology does resemble these secular institutions in that it provides a service in return for financial commitment and self-directed attendance support.

Anti-Authoritarianism

Mosocovici argues that postmodernity causes individuals to experience 'the fear of observed behaviour.'[120] Using the illustration of a child being coercively controlled by an adult to tidy their room by way of unremitting observation and threat of punishment, Giddens, citing Mosocovici's exemplification, contends that individuals similarly seek to avoid situations demanding compliance with social or institutional norms controlled by hierarchies.[121]

---

[118] BBC News, 'National Trust membership hits new high of five million,' (23 September 2017) accessed July 09, 2019, https://www.bbc.co.uk/news/uk-41361095.

[119] BBC News, 'Saving Pounds: the rise of the budget gym,' (16 July 2018) accessed July 09, 2019, https://www.bbc.co.uk/news/business-44766250.

[120] Pierre Moscovici in Gabriel Mugny and Juan Antonio Pérez, *The Social Psychology of Minority Influence*, European Monographs in Social Psychology (Cambridge: Cambridge University Press, 1991), 94.

[121] Anthony Giddens, ed., *Social Theory Today* (Cambridge: Polity Press, 1993), 72.

Leeman observes that ecclesiologies had historically moved toward centralised authority when Caesars ruled the world. However, during the revolutions of the 18th century, democratic governments proliferated and ecclesiologies have since been roughly matched by a corresponding proliferation of less hierarchical, but hierarchical nonetheless, forms of congregational governance. Reflecting our current anti-institution, anti-boundary, anti-authority age, he concludes that the de-institutionalisation and disintermediation of the church is inevitable, reflecting the postmodern values around which society is organised.[122] Leeman further contends that the primary problem confronting the church is that people crave relationship but, fuelled by a refusal to live according to another's stipulations, are fearful of any manifestation of authority within churches.[123] Consequently, if membership offers enhanced relationships without an institutionalised authoritarian ethos to underpin it, then such commitment will be less of an obstacle.[124]

Regretfully and too frequently, church membership is wrongly perceived and perfunctorily exercised for bureaucratic organisational purposes including hierarchical control, which heightens postmodernists' fears. Viola speaks of institutional churches which are constructed on programmes and rituals more than relationships, operating as if they exist above and beyond the people who populate them.[125] Such emphasis, he argues, discourages heart-

---

[122] Leeman, *The Church and the Surprising Offense of God's Love*, 39–41.
[123] Jonathan Duncan B. Forrester, William Storrar, and Andrew Morton, eds., *Public Theology for the 21st Century: Essays in Honour of Duncan B. Forrester* (London ; New York: T&T Clark, 2004), 406.
[124] This key issue will be further discussion in Chapter 5.
[125] Frank Viola, *Reimagining Church: Pursuing the Dream of Organic Christianity* (Colorado Springs: David C. Cook, 2008), 17–18.

commitment. Instead, Viola dreams of an organic church: 'authentic Christ-centred communities – where members know each other intimately, love one another unconditionally, bleed for one another deeply, and rejoice with one another unfailingly.'[126]

Some might argue this is an idealistic impossibility, a romanticised return to the Acts 2 model of church, failing to recognise that structures, which include somewhat authoritarian facets, are necessary to organise the contemporary church with all of its juridical commitments. However, the question remains: must intimate relationships and sound governance be mutually exclusive? Can Viola's dream, which is entirely dependent upon enduring spiritual renewal, be achieved within a diverse church demographic like ours? This question will be considered further in the chapters which follow.

Globalisation

Advances in technologies, hyper-mobilisation and communication in the milieu of consumerist, individualist, anti-authoritarian postmodern ideologies are facilitating people, companies and governments to become increasingly integrated, interactive and interconnected worldwide. 'For the first time in human history, the world is forging an awareness of our existence as a single entity.'[127] Guttal believes that globalisation will eventually construct such homogeneity that local and national economies integrate into one global, unregulated market economy.[128] Globalisation, however, is not exclusively an

---

[126] Frank Viola, *Reimaging Church*, 28.
[127] Leonard I. Sweet, Brian D. McLaren, and Jerry Haselmayer, *'A' Is for Abductive: The Language of the Emerging Church* (Grand Rapids: Zondervan, 2003), 138.
[128] Shalmali Guttal, *Globalisation: Development in Practice*, accessed October 11, 2019, www.jstor.org/stable/25548249.

economic process.

Ritzer was amongst the first to argue globalisation has socio-cultural aspects which leave an indelible 'McDonaldisation' mark on world religions.[129] Berger, once argued that globalisation, through exposure to variant ideologies and consequent homogenisation, would sound religions' death-knoll.[130] Retrospectively, blaming his atheist prejudices, he conceded he was mistaken, contending instead that humanity is capable of simultaneously sustaining globalisation and heterogeneous secular and religious institutions and associations.[131]

The paradox of globalisation's homogenous economic trajectory, despite socio-cultural heterogeneity, means church members cease to be solely reliant upon the teaching of their local church. Instead, they can electively scrutinise the local message against the ambiguous global smörgåsbord of online ideologies. Faith is no longer local, it is 'glocal,'[132] facilitating discipleship characterised by local and global considerations.[133] Morris concludes that globalisation, in the macro sense, simultaneously integrates and disintegrates the world[134] which, when applied to micro issues of commitment, has both negative and positive implications, especially if there is focal imbalance.

---

[129] George Ritzer, *The McDonaldization of Society 5* (Los Angles: Pine Forge Press, 2008), 1–22.

[130] Peter L Berger, *The Heretical Imperative: Contemporary Possibilities of Religious Affirmation* (Garden City: Anchor Press, 1980).

[131] Peter L. Berger, "Secularism in Retreat." *The National Interest* (December 01, 1996), 46.

[132] Roland Robertson is credited with coining this phrase. See Duncan B. Forrester, William Storrar, and Andrew Morton, eds., *Public Theology for the 21st Century: Essays in Honour of Duncan B. Forrester* (London: T&T Clark, 2004), 406.

[133] Rick Love, *GLOCAL: Following Jesus in the 21st Century* (Eugene: Cascade Books, 2017), 11-36.

[134] Morris, *Flexible Church*, 38–39.

Positively, individual members gain an expanded global consciousness beyond the minutia of local church issues. Negatively, pre-occupation with expanded horizons can minimise crucial missiological engagement locally.[135] 'A healthy glocal group of believers in this new century must be involved, at the same time, in God's mission locally and globally, that is glocally.'[136]

Homogenous Unit Principle

McGavran's 'homogenous unit principle' when considered alongside globalisation and postmodernism's egocentric tendencies, introduces further paradoxical abstruseness. McGavran argues that people prefer to experience faith without first needing to surmount sociological (more than theological) barriers, which might include geographical, ethnic, linguistic, social, educational, vocational, or economic factors, or a combination of several of these and other considerations.[137] He called this a 'homogenous unit,' defined as: 'a section of society in which all members have some characteristic in common.'

For Christians, this common characteristic is faith and baptism (Eph.4:5), or the Pauline concept of 'one mind' (Phil.2:2; 1 Cor.1:10). Novak argues that social, rather than spiritual commonality, causes groups subconsciously, sometimes consciously and even prejudicially, to build around themselves 'unmeltable ethnics' which stringently

---

[135] Tormod Engelsviken, Erling Lundeby, and Dagfinn Solheim, eds., *The Church Going Glocal: Mission and Globalisation ; [Proceedings of the Fjellhaug Symposium 2010]*, Regnum Edinburgh 2010 Series (Oxford: Regnum, 2011), 68–69.

[136] Craig Ott and Harold A. Netland, eds., *Globalizing Theology: Belief and Practice in an Era of World Christianity* (Grand Rapids: Baker Academic, 2006), 179.

[137] Tormod Engelsviken, Erling Lundeby, and Dagfinn Solheim, eds., *The Church Going Glocal: Mission and Globalisation,* 68–69.

structure humanity within similar categories.[138] Consequently, we tend to construct churches which exclude rather than include.

The formative nature of ethnic groups should not be underestimated: 'People have a tendency to gather together in groups to work, worship, play and socialise. Attitudes and views are expressed through such groups, and it is these group values and beliefs that determine the sort of people we are.'[139] As such, Ott and Netland contend that 'the local will always have a kind of priority over the global because...we are physically embodied creatures, inextricably rooted in particular localities.'[140] Rah rightly cautions that the Western Church must consciously comprehend the implications of such institutionalised homogeneity, especially since further globalisation will only cultivate increased secular pluralism and ethnic heterogeneity resulting in an unbiblical ecclesiology.[141]

Psychological Considerations

Distinct to the work of sociologists, psychology considers individual cognitive processing and consequent behaviour in reaction to contextualised situations.[142] Various theories will be considered before drawing ecclesiological conclusions from this socio-psychological analysis as they relate to membership.

---

[138] Michael Novak, *Unmeltable Ethnics: Politics & Culture in American Life*, 2nd ed (New Brunswick: Transaction, 1996), 46–48.
[139] Michael Novak, *Unmeltable Ethnics,* 10–16.
[140] Ott and Netland, *Globalizing Theology*, 21.
[141] Soong-Chan Rah, *The Next Evangelicalism: Releasing the Church from Western Cultural Captivity* (Downers Grove: IVP Books, 2009), 97–99. We will return to this theme in chapter 4.
[142] Kate Beaumont et al., *Introduction to Psychology* (Cape Town: Pearson Prentice Hall, 2007), 2–4.

Social Identity Theory

Paralleled to McGavran's HUP, Tajfel's 'Social Identity Theory' maintains that an individual's sense of identity is diametrically influenced by the group(s) to which they belong. Thus, the local church and the structures of which it is a part appreciably define our self-concept, including self-worth and self-esteem. Abrams calls this 'the group in the individual' which is implanted by being 'an individual in the group.'[143] Tajfel's thesis is that social identity is 'the knowledge that [one] belongs to certain social groups together with some emotional and value significance of...the group membership'[144] which disseminates specific normative, and therefore predictable, dynamics of group behaviour and attitude.

When applied to the church, Social Identity Theory hypothesises the direct correlation between the frequency and complexity of participation: the higher the frequency and more multifarious the involvement, the more profound commitment becomes.[145] Consequently, our SAGA generation, who tend to participate more due to a greater sense of 'in-ness,' would be more comfortable with Social Identity Theory's consequences. However, Social Identity Theory is conflictual for the pre-SAGA generation(s) because the transient/temporary nature of postmodernist existence would deem Social Identity Theory too restrictive and choice-limiting, and thus they participate less.

---

[143] Dominic Abrams, *Social Identifications: A Social Psychology of Intergroup Relations and Group Processes*. (New York: Routledge, 2016), 3.

[144] H.Tajfel in Dušan Kecmanović, *The Mass Psychology of Ethnonationalism*, PATH in Psychology (New York: Plenum Press, 1996), 29.

[145] John C. Turner in Henri Tajfel, ed., *Social Identity and Intergroup Relations*, European Studies in Social Psychology (Cambridge: Cambridge Univ. Press, 2010), 15–40.

Social Loafing

Secondly, Ringelmann's theory of 'social loafing' is pertinent. He proposes there is an inherent dissonance within individuals: if their contribution does not affect the outcome, they will become peripherally indifferent. Social loafing means individual commitment proportionately decreases as group size increases and consequently "others will do it" becomes the prevailing attitude.[146]

Local churches often experience this phenomenon as they grow numerically, especially amongst the pre-SAGA generation(s). In contrast, the SAGA generation, by and large, remains fully participative regardless of size. Ringelmann's theory would, therefore, promote ever-increasing responsibility within small(er) expressions of church (e.g. home groups, mentoring relationships, church/congregation plants, etc.). Otherwise, commitment from members reduces because they suppose their contribution is negligible and ineffective. The attitude of 'others will do it' might then be replaced with an attitude of 'this is my membership responsibility.' This issue will be further explored in Chapter 5.

Social Learning Theory

Thirdly, Bandura's Social Learning Theory argues that effective role models are essential because from them we establish (sub)cultural norms in a form of operant conditioning. Recurrent observation and subsequent imitation of such modelling reinforces the successes and failures of learning.[147] Needless to say, some role models are more influential than others. Assuming Bandura is right,

---

[146] Donelson R. Forsyth, *Group Dynamics* (Boston: Cengage, 2019), 313–19.
[147] Albert Bandura, *Social Learning Theory* (Englewood Cliffs: Prentice Hall, 1977), 37–41.

if we want the pre-SAGA generation(s) to take up influential roles (e.g. Leadership Team, small group leadership, mission or ministry leads, etc.), then the leadership we currently exercise must be conducive to such goals through effective mentoring, modelling and, crucially, an invitation to participate.[148] The theme of conducive leadership will be further considered in Chapter 5.

Socio-Psychological Theory Relating to Membership

The socio-psychological theories outlined above emphasise several factors which might variously influence degrees of commitment. Each can be associated explicitly or implicitly with the symptoms of Restaurant Ecclesiology. In summary, these theories are now drawn together.

Fichter's four membership typologies, which specifically hypothesise regarding the socio-cultural membership of religious institutions, insightfully distinguishes four membership typologies: the nuclear member (those who are most involved and faithful); the model member (those who are compliant with expected norms); the marginal member (those who are somewhat alienated or disaffected); and finally, the dormant member (those who are entirely disaffected or not practising faith).[149]

Classification within a specific typology, even if not wholly and in an overgeneralised sense, is determined by three psychological indicators: intention (the individual's self-perception of their association with the church); religious adherence (the degree of the individual's participation);

---

[148] This issue will be further considered in Chapter 5.

[149] In my specific local church context, 'dormant members' are annually reviewed and removed from our membership roll. As a consequence, there should not be an occasion where dormancy persists for more than 12-18 months, thus ensuring our membership is committed to Christ and the local church.

and, social participation (the individual's involvement in the organisational facets of church life).[150]

Based upon my interpretation, the majority of postmodern pre-SAGA generation(s) sit somewhere between the 'model' and 'marginal' member continuum, thus perpetuating Restaurant Ecclesiology. The SAGA generation is, typically, on a spectrum between the 'model' and 'nuclear' member which most church leaders would deem a healthy level of commitment for a member, as described in Chapter 2. It should, however, be noted that these classifications are not impermeable, transitional overlap occurs according to the fluctuating seasons of a person's life (e.g. health, availability, spiritual fervency, etc.).

Similar to Fichter and the theories of the other social scientists referenced, Lenski distinguishes between 'communal involvement' (those involved in the most influential areas of church life, typically the SAGA generation) and 'associated involvement' (those who merely attend church-related activities, typically the pre-SAGA generations). Lenski then further categorises individuals based upon 'doctrinal orthodoxy' (a 'hard' measurement of how much an individual subscribes to major Christian doctrines) and 'devotionalism' (a 'soft' measurement around the frequency of engagement with spiritual disciplines).[151] I will return to these essential aspects of discipleship in Chapter 4.

The above socio-psychological analysis and that which

---

[150] Joseph Henry Fichter, *Social Relations in the Urban Parish* (Chicago: Chicago University Press, 1954), 22-40.
[151] Gerhard Lenski, *The Religious Factor* (New York: Anchor Doubleday, 1963).

precedes it in Chapter 2 reiterates a question of a theological nature: what should commitment look like, not determined by societal views and conditions alone, but principally by God's will? This issue will be considered in the next chapter.

4 | Commitment and Covenant

Having identified the significance of covenantal theology in the founding ecclesiology of the Baptist church (Chapter 2), this chapter expands upon this theme, specifically exploring the Scriptural basis of covenants more generally, having first acknowledged the undulating significance of covenants during the 20th century. In response, the contemporary value of covenants will be evaluated, markedly seeking resolution to the problems presented by Restaurant Ecclesiology amongst the pre-SAGA generation(s) by coining a new phrase to augment the original meaning of covenant commitment. Could such recovery, or at least reframing, positively influence the detrimental socio-psychological symptoms highlighted in Chapter 3? Furthermore, would a rediscovery of the language of covenant go some way to establish a new ecclesiological metaphor (Chapter 5)?

Defining Covenant
Cross states, 'Oath and covenant is...a widespread legal means by which duties and privileges of kinship may be extended to another individual or group, including

aliens.'[152] The familial connection of kinship is significant. Cross, alongside Glueck,[153] Hahn[154] and Frymer-Kensky[155] recognise that kinship, or a depth of connection, performs a stabilising function of covenant relationship before establishment or as a consequent result of it; covenant additionally involves a dutiful and rightful commitment within this relationship. Summarising the scholars above, in what follows I maintain that covenants are best understood as 'bilateral, relational commitments with privileges and responsibilities, usually formalised, between one or more parties.'

Covenantal Theology Amongst Baptists

As previously stated in Chapter 2, and necessarily explored given my context, Baptists have historically referred to their covenantal model of association as 'walking together.' Jackson elucidates that covenantal theology was consistently practised amongst Baptists since inception. However, he notes a dramatic shift in emphasis during the 20th century: covenant ecclesiology, especially in solemnised corroborated forms, begins to play second fiddle (or less) to other increasingly prominent themes. Consequently, it was these other themes which became the defining marks of what it meant to be identified to Christ

---

[152] Frank Moore Cross, *From Epic to Canon: History and Literature in Ancient Israel*, Johns Hopkins, A Johns Hopkins Paperback (Baltimore: The Johns Hopkins Univ. Press, 2000), 3–4.

[153] Nelson Glueck, *Hesed in the Bible* (Eugene: Wipf & Stock Publishers, 2011), 39-45.

[154] Scott Hahn, *Kinship by Covenant: A Canonical Approach to the Fulfillment of God's Saving Promises*, The Anchor Yale Bible Reference Library (New Haven: Yale University Press, 2009), 28.

[155] Victor Harold Matthews, Bernard M Levinson, and Tikva Simone Frymer-Kensky, *Gender and Law in the Hebrew Bible and the Ancient Near East* (London: T & T Clark, 2004), 11.

Commitment and Covenant 61

and his people.[156] The declining prominence of covenantal theology, at least denominationally, is most noticeably identified by contrasting founding Baptist principles with those published throughout the 20th century.

In 1912, the first edition of 'Baptist Principles,' outlining the basis of understanding and subsequent enactment for all who belong to the Baptist Union, contains just two pages regarding 'covenant,' against forty-six pages devoted to the new dominant theme of baptism, including a weighty section provocatively entitled 'Return to Believers' Baptism.'[157] By contrast, the equivalent 1607 founding document prioritises the primary significance of a bilateral, cruciform, covenantal relationship as *the* distinctive 'visible' mark of Baptist identity: 'The outward part of the true forme of the true visible church is a vowe, promise, oath, or covenant betwixt God and the Saints.'[158]

In a thorough examination of this theme, Jackson identifies that this downward prioritisation of covenant continued in future editions of 'Baptist Principles,' alongside other publications by prominent denominational authors. For example, the post-war Union report, 'The Doctrine of the Church,' largely excludes any reference to covenant.[159] In 1953, responding to the prevailing issue of church

---

[156] Darrell Richard Jackson, "The Covenantal Discourse of Contemporary Baptist Belonging and Membership," in *The Discourse of 'Belonging' and Baptist Church Membership In Contemporary Britain: Historical, Theological and Demotic Elements of a Post-Foundational Theological Proposal*, (Birmingham: University of Birmingham, 2009), 68-92.

[157] The earliest version was included in C.E. Shipley, *The Baptists of Yorkshire* (1912), accessed June 29, 2019,

https://files.huddersfield.exposed/localhistory/books/The%20Baptists%20of%20 Yorkshire%20(1912)%20%5bLQ%20yale.39002085618248%5d.pdf.

[158] W.T.Whitley, *The Works of John Smyth: Fellow of Christ's College, 1594-8,* Volume 1 (Cambridge: Cambridge University Press, 1915), 254.

[159] Darrell Richard Jackson, *The Discourse of Belonging,* 69.

governance, Cook makes only passing reference to covenant in a circumscribing publication entitled 'What Baptists Stand For.'[160]

Davie argues that before the Great Wars, belief without belonging was considered a paradoxical misnomer since belief without belonging is incomplete. Post-war, however, the demographic, sociological, political and economic reorganisation of Europe resulted in a seismic shift in the relationship between belief and practice, especially relative to expression within institutionalised religion. Belief was high, but practice, expressed through participative membership in institutional religions, was low.[161]

In 1963, Gilmore's publication 'The Pattern of the Church: A Baptist View' extols the significance of baptism for forty pages and obliquely mentions 'covenant' twice.[162] Tellingly, Jackson identifies that three of the four sections in 'Baptist Principles' that same decade describe features of membership and yet no reference is made to covenant being intrinsic. He contends that charismatic renewal, controversy around modes of leadership and the circumvention of life-threatening denominational decline became the dominant focuses in the 1970s.[163]

As this brief survey of my own context thus far emphasises, the significance of covenantal theology consciously diminishes in Baptist thinking and practice during the 20th

---

[160] H.Cook, *What Baptists Stand For* (London: Carey Kingsgate Press, 1953), 48-49.
[161] Grace Davie, *Religion in Britain since 1945: Believing without Belonging*, Making Contemporary Britain (Oxford: Blackwell, 1994), 1–9.
[162] A.Gilmore, *The Pattern of the Church: A Baptist View,* (London: Lutterworth Press, 1963).
[163] Darrell Richard Jackson, *The Discourse of 'Belonging*, 68-92.

century. Jackson contends that the underplaying of covenant over other themes, chiefly baptism, is unsurprising since the change of emphasis coincided with an unprecedented period in post-war history which sought convergence between the Christian traditions: 'The theological exploration of baptism offered a substantially larger number of points of contact with the baptismal practices and theologies of the other Christian traditions than would an emphasis on covenant.'[164]

The 1980s heralded a forceful call to return to covenantal relationships by several prominent Baptist theologians, however. For example, Haymes, arguing against postmodernism, stated: 'we [Baptists] must shift our thinking away from our over-active, self-assertion, to the God who makes covenant in Christ.'[165] Other theologians propagated similar concern: 'the image of the covenant...which used to play such a luminous part within the Baptist tradition...today, alas, is barely appreciated in its depth and richness, if at all.'[166] Not everyone agreed. For example, Campbell stated that peripheral issues, notably covenant, were being championed at the centre by a fringe minority: 'The question of Baptist identity does not greatly bother...most people in the churches.'[167] Campell's contention, symptomatic of the prevailing postmodern worldview accentuated in Chapter 3, was that Baptist identity was constituently considered an unnecessary

---

[164] Darrell Richard Jackson, *The Discourse of 'Belonging*, 70.
[165] B.Haymes, "On Being the Church" in *A Call to Mind: Baptist Essays towards a theology of Commitment.* (London: The Baptist Union of Great Britain, 1981), 67.
[166] P.S. Fiddes, R. Hayden, R.L. Kidd, et al. (eds.), *Bound to Love: the Covenant Basis of Baptist Life and Mission* (London: The Baptist Union, 1985), 5.
[167] A.Campbell, 'The Grounds of Association' in D.Slater (ed.) *A Perspective on Baptist Identity* (Kingsbridge: Mainstream, 1987), 7.

categorisation when expressing identity with Christ.

During the 1990s, when postmodernist ideologies where most assiduously gaining traction in the church, Fiddes argued that, in continuity with our historical past, 'covenant', 'fellowship' and 'Body' could be especially helpful in seeking to understand the theological basis of union between Christian churches in general and Baptist churches in particular.[168] At the turn of the millennium, a denominational consultation entitled 'Theology and a Baptist Way of Community,' which was an attempt by the Union to popularise covenant ecclesiology, emphasised 'the experience of being part of a Baptist community of worship and mission rather than making a list of Baptist Principles.'[169] Similarly, Finamore optimistically argued, 'We have a theological theme that was of central importance for several centuries, and is gradually being recovered in our day...the idea of covenant...which took particular form in our own church life....[and which] stands at the beginning of our story.'[170] Weaver contended that covenant was 'at the heart of renewing relationships...and at the heart of all our reforms, whatever shape they take.'[171]

In 2001, a resource was published in response to these and other voices called 'Covenant 21.' The vision of Covenant 21 concerned the covenantal rediscovery and prioritisation

---

[168] Paul.S.Fiddes, *The Nature of the Assembly and the Council of the Baptist Union of Great Britain*, (Didcot: The Baptist Union of Great Britain, 1994), 4.

[169] P.S. Fiddes, B.Haymes, B.Kidd, et al. (eds.) 'Theology and a Baptist Way of Community' in *Doing Theology in a Baptist Way* (Oxford: Whitley Publications, 2000), 23.

[170] Stephen Finamore, in A.Clarke (ed.) "Baptists in Covenant" in *Bound for Glory? God, Church and World in Covenant* (Oxford: Whitley Publications, 2002), 84.

[171] John Weaver in S.Murray (ed.), "Translocal Leadership: A Theological Reflection" in *Translocal Ministry: 'equipping the churches for mission'* (Didcot: The Baptist Union of Great Britain, 2004), 54.

of 'the spiritual relationship over the institutional relationship'[172] with God and one another. Most recently, in 2016, Green repeated the call to rediscover covenant commitment.[173]

These prominent advocates, however, have failed to be heard beyond a minority of leaders having a specific interest in Baptist identity. Consequently, contemporary practice continues to minimise the practice of covenant, as described in Chapter 2, and significantly, our model constitutions neither reference nor require them. Jackson contends that the majority of Baptists, especially those without formal theological education, consider such matters 'archaic, even unfathomable.'[174] Hayden concluded that the influence of postmodernism was to blame.[175]

Based upon my socio-psychological research (Chapter 3), I expect a combination of these and various other factors, including pure pragmatism and the prioritisation of missional matters while managing indefatigable judicial requirements, all perceived as more pressing, are to blame. Covenantal theology, therefore, still has some way to go before it can claim widespread denominational acceptance, but is this right given biblical teaching and Baptist assertions of having a biblically precedented ecclesiology?

---

[172] The Baptist Union of Great Britain, *Covenant 21: Covenant for a Gospel People*, (The Baptist Union: Didcot, 2001), 2.
[173] Lynn Green, "Renewing The Covenant," *Baptists Together: the magazine for the Baptist Union of Great Britain*, (Spring 2016): 6-8.
[174] Darrell Richard Jackson, *The Discourse of Belonging*, 91.
[175] R.Hayden in "The Mutation of Calvinism" in M.Blyth (ed.), *Joined-up Thinking: Membership* (Didcot: The Baptist Union of Great Britain, 2004), 12.

Covenants In Scripture

Examples of covenant-making can be identified throughout the ancient world. These covenants, wherever used, are characteristic in form, typically including an introductory preamble; followed by a historical review of the relationship; a series of stipulations to determine the obligation; and, finally, a list of consequences for breaking the agreement. The covenant was usually ceremonially solemnised.[176] God similarly established conditional ("if, then I will") and unconditional ("I will") promissory covenants, to mediate a personal relationship with his people to communicate: 'I will be your God and you shall be my people' (Lev.6:12; 2 Cor.6:16).[177]

In the broadest sense, throughout the Old Testament, God uses covenants to identify his people and establish his kingdom.[178] The same theme is consistent: God promises His commitment and protection in return for Israel's pledge of fidelity, including the upholding of moral and social standards (e.g. Deut.28:15-19). In the New Testament, God establishes a more effectual covenant in and through Christ as the foundation for the Church.[179]

The Bible uses just two words for 'covenant' which occur 316 times in 295 verses.[180] In the Old Testament, *běriyth* (derived from the word 'cut') means a covenant, alliance,

---

[176] Max Weber, *Ancient Judaism* (London: Collier Macmillan Publishers, 2014), 3–60.
[177] Jonathan Leeman, *The Church and the Surprising Offense of God's Love*, 235–39.
[178] For a summary of Old Testament covenants, see Appendix A.
[179] Jonathan Leeman, *The Church and the Surprising Offense of God's Love*, 239–47.
[180] James Strong, *Strong's Exhaustive Concordance of the Bible* (Peabody: Hendrickson Pub., 2012), H1285 and G1242.

pledge, treaty, league, constitution, and an agreement.[181] Pertinent to the focus of this book, Hugenberger emphasises that Old Testament covenant-making customarily included eating together as a sign of unity (Gen.26:30, 31:51-54; Ex.24:1-11).[182] In the New Testament, *diathēkē* means: a disposition, arrangement, covenant, testament or will.[183]

Williamson argues that God uses covenants to achieve two primary goals: broadly speaking to establish his kingdom rule among a people identified with himself and explicitly to distinguish people from the prevailing culture.[184] Simply stated, as Gushee argues, a covenant takes faithless people and exhorts them to keep faith: 'Covenants are God's way of organising, sustaining, and reclaiming relationships established in creation but damaged by sin.'[185] My purpose here is not a detailed analysis of the different covenants or how covenants were made, but rather to highlight that covenants are consistently prominent in Scripture.[186]

The New Covenant

The Old Testament covenants[187] form the basis of the 'Old Covenant'. However, despite significant spiritual revival under Josiah (2 Ki.22-23), most unambiguously through

---

[181] James Strong, *Strong's Exhaustive Concordance*, H1285.
[182] Gordon P Hugenberger, *Marriage as a Covenant: Biblical Law and Ethics as Developed from Malachi* (Eugene: Wipf & Stock, 2014), 205–6.
[183] James Strong, *Strong's Exhaustive Concordance*, G1242.
[184] Paul R. Williamson, *Sealed with an Oath: Covenant in God's Unfolding Purpose*, New Studies in Biblical Theology 23 (Downers Grove: Apollos/InterVarsity Press, 2007), 75–76.
[185] David P. Gushee, *In the Fray: Contesting Christian Public Ethics, 1994-2013* (Eugene: Cascade Books, 2014), 82, 88.
[186] For a thorough description of covenants in Scripture, see Peter John Gentry and Stephen J. Wellum, *God's Kingdom through God's Covenants: A Concise Biblical Theology* (Wheaton: Crossway, 2015).
[187] For a summary of Old Testament covenants, see Appendix A.

Jeremiah (Jer.2:5-11, 32:30) and various other prophets (Isa.55:3, 59:21, 61:8-9; Eze.16:60, 34:25-31, 37:26-28; cf. Ro.11:25-27; Heb.8:7-9:1, 10:16-17), God announces his desire for a genuine, lasting and irreversible reform. A 'New Covenant' would permanently reconcile humanity to God (Jer.31:31-34), mediated by Christ through his death on the cross (Lk.2:20), which is celebrated as the metanarrative in the pages of the New Testament.

The confusing ambiguity of conditional and unconditional, lateral and unilateral, literal and metaphorical strands of the Old Testament covenants synergise and find fulfilment in Christ. Through Christ, the Mosaic Law is fulfilled (Mt.5:17): 'God fulfils all his promises and deals with the results of human failure to keep our obligation.'[188] Hebrews 8 explains how this Christ mediates his New Covenant, founded upon superior promises to the Old Testament covenants (Heb.8:6-13). Hebrews 9 describes how Christ has obtained eternal redemption (Heb.9:11-28), thus, enabling humanity to serve the living God in advance of his return (Heb.9:28).

The New Covenant amplifies the blessing aspect of the Abrahamic Covenant, particularly concerning salvation, ultimately replacing the Law aspects of the Mosaic Covenant (Jer.31:31-32; Ro.6:14-15). Prophesying the New Covenant, Ezekiel exhorts several benefits (a new heart, a new spirit, true holiness and the indwelling Spirit) which Paul states the Mosaic Law could not provide (Ez.36:24-28; cf. Ro.3:20). Following the resurrection of Christ, Gentiles were brought into this blessing (Ac.10; Eph.2:13-14) and the fulfilment of the New Covenant will be seen on earth and ultimately and eternally, in heaven.

---

[188] The Baptist Union of Great Britain, *Covenant 21*, 5

The Church Grafted Into The Covenantal Storyline

For this book, an essential point must be noted: the Scriptures connect the New Covenant with the Church (or Body of believers), of which Christ is the Head, the vehicle through which he, as Priest and mediator, will fulfil the New Covenant (Mt.26:28; Mk.14:24; Lk.22:14-20; 1 Cor.11:25; 2 Cor.3:6; Heb.7:22, 8:6-13, 9:15, 10:16, 29, 12:24, 13:20).[189]

Significantly, this New Covenant, like the Old Testament ratification of covenants, symbolises unity through eating together: 'You embraced us as your children and welcomed us to sit and eat with you.'[190] The Old Testament covenants were a shadow of what was to come (Heb.1:5, 8-9,13), something which Paul understood (e.g. Ro.4:13-16).

Establishing continuity with the past, Jesus, as 'the last Adam,' 'the Son of David,' 'the new Israel' and 'the seed of Abraham' (1 Cor.15:22; cf. Lk.3:23-38) speaks of the 'covenant in my blood' which includes a continuous call into the covenant he established: 'Do this in remembrance of me' (Lk.22:19; cf. 1 Cor.11:22-23). As Carson argues, Jesus' use of this phrase is the antitype to the type of Exodus 24:8 since his incarnational life and death would supersede the debt incurred under the Old Covenant (Rom.3:25-26; Col.1:13; Heb.9:15, 10:10).[191] 'He [Jesus] was alluding backwards to God's promise through Jeremiah...[and] alluding forward to the death he was about to undergo.'[192]

---

[189] Space does not allow for a full discussion of differing views relating to the New Covenant and the Church. For a detailed discussion of the eschatological implications, see Homer A. Kent, "The New Covenant And The Church," in *Grace Theological Journal*, 6.2 (1985) 289-298.

[190] Church of England, ed., *Common Worship: Services and Prayers for the Church of England* (London: Church House Publ, 2000), Communion Service Prayer H.

[191] D.A. Carson in Gushee, *In the Fray*, 83–85.

[192] Jonathan Leeman, *The Church and the Surprising Offense of God's Love,* 241.

Christ, as Head of the Body (1 Cor.11:3; Eph.1:22, 4:15, 5:23; Col.1:18, 2:10, 19) has become and remains the covenantal head over Christians individually and corporately (as the New Covenant people of Christ, the Church). Christ and individual believers are united within this one Body. Thus, the 'Christian life necessarily has a congregational shape;'[193] moreover, any definition of the church as an expression of his kingdom, Leeman argues, must begin with Christ's covenant which has explicit and unbroken continuity with the Old Covenant back to his original purposes in Eden.[194]

As we have seen, covenants have been used in every stage of redemptive history to affirm identity and establish relationship. Leeman speaks of the New Covenant being a threefold union: firstly, representationally (Ro.5:12-21) which is a formal commitment for us to share in his life, death, burial, resurrection, ascension, rule, and reign. As Ferguson argues, this means that 'all he has done for me, representatively becomes mine actually.'[195] Secondly, spiritually, because we have been given his Spirit (1 Cor.12:13; cf. Rom.8:9-11; 1 Cor.6:17-19; 1 Jn.3:24, 4:13) which is a sign that Christ's New Covenant is active. Thirdly, the New Covenant unites the Church to Christ by faith (Jn.2:11, 3:16; Ro.10:14; Gal.2:16; Phil.1:29) which is the only means (as argued in Chapter 2) by which individuals can be saved.[196] The implications of this threefold covenantal union are: (1) members of the church share identity with one another (including work, relationships,

---

[193] Jonathan Leeman, *The Church and the Surprising Offense of God's Love*, 245.
[194] Jonathan Leeman, *The Church and the Surprising Offense of God's Love*, 241–42.
[195] Sinclair B Fergusson, *The Holy Spirit*. (Leicester: IVP, 1996), 109.
[196] Jonathan Leeman, *The Church and the Surprising Offense of God's Love*, 243–47.

joys and sorrows (e.g. 1 Cor.12:26); (2) Christians must not remain aloof from a local church since, (3) individual believers, as regenerate, Spirit-filled recipients of Jesus' covenant grace, are unilaterally included within the Body which has participative implications for integration locally.[197] So, we should join local churches, Bray argues, because 'it is an essential part of the identity of individual Christians' and therefore our 'primary community'[198] which comes with mutually affirmed rights and responsibilities.

The central question in this chapter is whether, as local churches, we should embrace a traditional covenantal theology, a progressive dispensational theology partially determined by contemporary worldviews or a path between. As argued, the theme of 'covenant' runs throughout the Scriptures and has universal theological and ecclesiological continuity which extends to the contemporary Church. Therefore, my conclusion is that, as a theological imperative, covenantal ecclesiology similar to founding Baptist principles, should be pursued. As identified, however, this would be a tough assignment given contemporary associations with the conception of covenant. Perhaps the coining of a new word or phrase, which has etymological integrity with covenant commitment, might reframe the concept, and, if it is so 'archaic, even unfathomable,'[199] may even redeem it.

Moynagh argues that sound ecclesiology is inherently relational/directional: relationship with God (up, what I call vertical); Christ-followers relationships with each other (in,

---

[197] Jonathan Leeman, *The Church and the Surprising Offence of God's Love*, 245–47.
[198] Gerald Lewis Bray, *The Church*, 249.
[199] Darrell Richard Jackson, *The Discourse of Belonging*, 91.

what I call horizontal); relationships beyond the church (out, expressed in our desire for augmented community connectedness); and connection with the broader church (of).[200] Leeman cautions regarding the evangelical trend towards over-emphasising the missional nature of the church which, he argues, can become reductionistic in that the church becomes little more than a functionary body. Before we can be useful in mission, we need first to grasp whom God has made us to be in Christ individually and together (i.e. 2 Cor.8:5).

As Guder argues, to be light to the world, 'It means, first of all [after union with Christ], that the inner, communal life of the church matters for mission.'[201] As such, the coining of any new word must necessarily recapture the essence of these elements without over or understating the vertical commitment, (which is principal), at the expense of the horizontal commitment and vice versa.

Frequently, the church errs to one side of the pendulum over the other. Any new word/phrase must hold in tension the extremes of being a consumer (who only takes) or excessively contributes (and never receives). Starkly stated, I feel there is a fluctuating imbalance in membership in both directions, whereby members feel it is their right to consume and leaders feel the compulsion to control. Unhelpfully, many church constitutions, especially in Baptist circles, promote this imbalance (e.g. the leadership cannot remove members; members perceive leaders primarily as 'servants,' etc.). Leeman argues that covenant

---

[200] Michael Moynagh and Philip Harrold, *Church for Every Context: An Introduction to Theology and Practice* (London: SCM Press, 2012), 435–36.
[201] Darrell L. Guder and Lois Barrett, eds., *Missional Church: A Vision for the Sending of the Church in North America*, The Gospel and Our Culture Series (Grand Rapids: W.B. Eerdmans Pub, 1998), 128.

powerfully, when properly understood, involves, for all parties, a commitment of the whole person in such a dramatic fashion that dedication to Christ and all of Christ's people becomes our very identity.[202] Therefore, 'Church covenants make membership meaningful because they clarify the spiritual and relational commitments that membership signifies,'[203] keeping nominalism away while unambiguously promoting mutual accountability.

Membership makes the invisible visible; the association with the intangible universal is perceptibly expressed through participation locally:[204] 'the new covenant of Christ embraces an individual silently and invisibly...but...Christ intended this covenant to show up on earth.'[205] 'Anything less than a conscious commitment to the important is an unconscious commitment to the unimportant.'[206]

Towards A New Phrase

Lexicographer, McKean, champions the creation of new words/concepts to restate that which might otherwise be lost through language evolution. She argues that a new word, mutually understood, arrests the attention of those who would otherwise not take notice, overcomes atrophy and unlocks troves of fascinating information. She states that six principles must, however, be followed.[207] New

---

[202] Jonathan Leeman, *The Church and the Surprising Offense of God's Love*, 249–50.
[203] Mark Dever and Paul Alexander, *The Deliberate Church: Building Your Ministry on the Gospel* (Wheaton: Crossway Books, 2005), 62.
[204] Jonathan Leeman, *The Church and the Surprising Offense of God's Love*, 267.
[205] Jonathan Leeman, *The Church and the Surprising Offense of God's Love*, 268.
[206] Stephen R. Covey, A. Roger Merrill, and Rebecca R. Merrill, *First Things First: To Live, to Love, to Learn, to Leave a Legacy* (New York: Free Press, 2003), 32.
[207] Erin McKean, *"Go Ahead, Make Up New Words!,"* TED Talks, 2014, accessed July 15, 2019,
https://www.ted.com/talks/erin_mckean_go_ahead_make_up_new_words.

words can be: borrowed or stolen from other languages,[208] compounded,[209] blended,[210] shifted in function,[211] shortened[212] and/or acronymed.[213] Using these principles, I have coined a new word/phrase, '*koinocovenantal commitment,*' which seeks to redeem and communicate the inseparable concept of covenant with commitment and vice versa while maintaining etymological integrity.[214]

Koinocovenantal Commitment

This new phrase, 'koinocovenantal commitment' (with or without '-al'), conveys the cruciform, God-ward and other-ward, nature of relationships captured in biblical covenants. My conviction is that 'koinocovenant' is inseparable from 'commitment' since covenant necessitates promises and commitments; otherwise, it is an inadequate expression, potentially causing two parties (church and members) to be moving in different directions. Under such circumstances, they will not experience *koinonia*. Therefore, 'koinocovenant(al) commitment' perfectly expresses the complementary wholeness of covenant and commitment without compromising its original meaning.[215]

Koinocovenantal commitment can be used as an adjective, noun or verb. The ability to shift the function of the new word is subtle but noteworthy, accentuating that the

---

[208] e.g. The word 'ninja' is a Japanese word. 'Caramel' is borrowed from the French.

[209] e.g. 'heartbroken' or 'bookworm' or 'sandcastle.'

[210] e.g. The words 'lunch' and 'breakfast' are compounded to make the word 'brunch.' 'Motor' and 'hotel' are compounded to make the word 'motel.'

[211] e.g. 'Friend' used to be a noun but is now also used as a verb. 'Commercial' used to be an adjective but is now also a noun.

[212] e.g. The word 'edit' has been formed from the word 'editor.'

[213] e.g. 'National Aeronautics and Space Administration' becomes 'NASA.'

[214] See Appendix B to understand the etymological methodology employed.

[215] See Appendix B for the etymological methodology leading to the coining of 'koinocovenant(al) commitment.'

Church is more than a verb 'go,' it is a noun which has a distinct love and unity (e.g. John 13:35). In other words, the effectiveness of the church outwardly is inextricably linked to who we are internally (Eph. 3:10) which is effective proportionate only to our primary vertical (God-ward) commitment (2 Cor.8:5).

This new phrase, in addition to providing a replacement metaphor to understand local church ecclesiology (Chapter 5), could recover something of the essential nature of covenant commitment, especially amongst the pre-SAGA generation(s) but equally further entrench commitment amongst the SAGA-generation.

5 | Family Table Ecclesiology

In this chapter, a replacement ecclesiological metaphor for Restaurant Ecclesiology will be advocated, within which *koinocovenantal commitment* can be efficaciously expressed, seeking to confront postmodern challenges associated with the pre-SAGA generation(s). It is hoped that the new metaphor will transcend mere academic comprehension of the issues, becoming an applicatory tool to change ecclesiological thinking at an unconscious level within the local church. As Peterson argues, 'An abstract truth makes a wonderful poster.'[216]

Identifying A New Ecclesiological Metaphor

During two decades of leadership, innumerable strategies, with varying success, have been episodically employed in an attempt to subjugate the negative aspects of Restaurant Ecclesiology, including: teaching around the doctrine of the Church; delivering programmes to release gifting, including targeted development of young(er) leaders; exhorting the rights and responsibilities of membership; variously raising and lowering commitment expectations; etc. The primary

---

[216] Eugene Peterson, *Working The Angles: The Shape of Pastoral Integrity* (Grand Rapids: Eerdmans, 1987), 133.

focus throughout was numerical growth and augmented missional engagement, alongside prioritising spiritual growth, which we anticipated would increase the commitment of members as described in Chapter 2. At no point in this journey, however, were covenants introduced beyond the verbal affirmation of our '2Cs of Membership' described in Chapter 1.

Retrospectively, it is evident that the majority of this effort has been, returning to the Restaurant Ecclesiology metaphor, akin to shifting and amalgamating tables, adjusting the menu to meet differing tastes and/or refurbishing the establishment around engrained consumeristic principles. By God's sovereign grace, we have more 'loyal customers,' a larger 'waiting team' to accommodate the growth, and there has been kingdom fruit. Nevertheless, commitment from the ever-growing pre-SAGA generation(s) compared to the organically decreasing SAGA generation continues to be less than we consider appropriate. Consequently, the troubling sense that there must be a better way persists. The restaurant industry offers a partial metaphorical solution in the form of communal sharing tables.

Communal Sharing Tables

Over recent years, contrary to the values of postmodernity, restaurateurs reintroduced[217] 'sharing tables,' propagated around the myth that eating-out is an increasingly sociable activity amongst strangers. Anthropologists have noticed a

---

[217] Communal tables were commonplace in Europe until the mid-1800s, after which separate tables were introduced. Surprisingly, diners reported that these private tables were 'unquestionably difficult to get used to' because eating alone felt like a 'transgression against social norms.' See Gillian Crowther, *Eating Culture: An Anthropological Guide to Food* (Toronto: University of Toronto Press, 2018), 186.

thought-provoking socio-psychological trend in the West however, which is consistent with my conclusions in Chapter 3: these communal tables are never the first to be occupied.[218] Instead, customers prefer to be seated alone or in private groups, only accepting communal tables when other options are exhausted. Critics argue that restaurateurs persist with sharing tables, not for the stated reason of conviviality, but for a pragmatic economic reason: increased seating capacity.[219] In actuality, the eating experience at sharing tables remains an impersonal commercial transaction since those who involuntarily frequent communal tables with strangers are alone together in an atmosphere of unexpressed 'agreeable abandon.'[220] 'Alone together in agreeable abandon' has synergy with the symptoms of Restaurant Ecclesiology and could retrospectively provide an overstated definition for the symptoms of postmodernism.

Despite consumer apathy towards sharing tables, I wish to borrow the concept for my new ecclesiological metaphor. However, to avoid the mutually shared Restaurant Ecclesiology problem of people analogously eating 'alone together in agreeable abandon,' the location of my metaphorical 'sharing table' is most significant. I plan to move it from a 'restaurant' into a 'family home.' Such relocation is meaningful, since in its new environment the nature of interpersonal interaction and roles for 'diners' and 'waiting staff' alike are redefined, simultaneously and organically promoting the rights and responsibilities the

---

[218] Gillian Crowther, *Eating Culture,* 191–92.

[219] Alison Pearlman, *Smart Casual: The Transformation of Gourmet Restaurant Style in America* (Chicago: University of Chicago Press, 2013), 1–10.

[220] Rebecca L. Spang, *The Invention of the Restaurant: Paris and Modern Gastronomic Culture*, Harvard Historical Studies 135 (Cambridge: Harvard University Press, 2001), 242.

new location mandates: 'diners' become 'family members' and 'waiting staff' are concurrently affirmed as family and 'hosts.'

(Re)Employing The Family and Family Table Metaphors

The enduring appropriateness of the family and family-table metaphors cannot be overstated biblically and theologically. If my replacement ecclesiological metaphor is to have longevity, familial language needs to be redeemed in local contexts, remembering that regenerate believers are eternally adopted as 'sons and daughters' into the family of God (Ro.8:14-17, 9:8, 25-26; Gal.4:4-7; Eph.1:3, 13-14; 1 Jn.3:1-2). Paul uses the family metaphor to communicate the expectation that faith and maturity will grow within this profound context (Eph.4:11-16), while honouring Christ as our Elder 'brother' (Mt.12:50; Ro.8:29; Heb.2:11; cf. Mk.3:32-35) and God as Father (e.g. Ro.8:17; Eph.3:14; 1 Jn.3:1), experiencing the revelation of God's grace and mercy (Eph.1:5-6). Furthermore, other believers become mutually accountable spiritual siblings (Mt.18:15; Jn.1:12). The apostles also cherished the metaphor(s), often using familial language (e.g. Tit.2:1-8; 1 Jn.2:12-14), with an accompanying call to relate to one another within the household or family of God (1 Tim.3:15, 5:1-2).

Therefore, it would be more beneficial in the future if our ecclesiology were consciously interpreted, organised and experienced around a family sharing table, in a family home, rather than around individual or communal restaurant tables. Leeman argues, 'we do not attend a family meal simply because there is good food on offer, we do so because of who we are – members of the family, brought together through relationship with Christ.'[221] As

---

[221] Jonathan Leeman, *The Church and the Surprising Offense of God's Love*, 136.

Leeman's thesis implies, the aspirations of legitimate family members should not, therefore, be symptomatic of the postmodern values described in Chapter 3.

Family Table Ecclesiology

The 'family table' metaphor provides a foundation upon which members, especially the pre-SAGA generation(s), can gain a renewed perception of their familial identity, and, a fresh appreciation of what it means to belong and express that belonging through participation. I have called this replacement metaphor 'Family Table Ecclesiology'.

The sharing of a table has the potential for a sincere human connection. Around the family table, we encounter those we love (and those we sometimes struggle to love). A family table is a place where meals are lovingly served; stories can be told; worries, memories, confessions and dreams are revealed; praying, laughing, rejoicing and weeping is permissible (Ro.15:15). The table, whatever its size, can be a place of physical and spiritual nourishment, even challenge; renewal, reconciliation and revelation; building community and a place for mission and service which disturbs social norms and exclusivism (Mt.11:18-19; cf. Deut.21:20).[222] The family table accommodates and nurtures the different maturation stages of the generations, while clarifying roles and responsibilities.

Smith suggests that table fellowship replicates something intrinsic to the incarnational ministry of Christ: 'Eating was for Jesus a key means by which he proclaimed the coming

---

[222] John Franklin Koenig, *New Testament Hospitality: Partnership with Strangers as Promise and Mission* (Eugene: Wipf and Stock, 2001), 17–20.

of God's reign and acted, or enacted its arrival.'[223] Wright similarly promotes the significance of table sharing in Christ's ministry, contending that when Jesus wanted to explain about his forthcoming death to his disciples, he did so around a meal.[224]

In the Old Testament and New Testament, the table of Passover and the table of Communion are powerfully symbolic to the spiritual lives of God's people as a means of grace. Luke particularly repeatedly emphasises the significance of meals in Jesus' ministry (Lk.5:27-39, 7:36-50, 9:10-17, 10:38-42, 11:37-54, 14:1-24, 19:1-10, 22:7-23, 24:13-35, 24:36-53). Substantially, Scripture records many of Jesus' teaching illustrations focused on meal tables (e.g. Mt.11:18-19, 15:20, 22:2-14, 24:38, 25:1-13; Lk.10:7, 11:5-12, 12:36, 13:26, 14:16-24, 17:8; Jn.4:31-34, 6:25-59).

Reflecting upon Isaiah's Old Testament eschatological prophecy, which includes a family feast (Isa.25:6), Pohl argues, 'A shared meal is the activity most closely tied to the reality of God's kingdom, just as it is the most basic expression of hospitality.'[225] As Bartchy contends, it is not inconsequential or unintentional that Jesus explicitly connects his 'last supper' with the New Covenant (Lk.21:20) and subsequently encourages his disciples to follow his example in remembrance as the fullest expression of *koinonia* (Lk.22:19).[226]

---

[223] Gordon T. Smith, *A Holy Meal: The Lord's Supper in the Life of the Church* (Grand Rapids, Mich: Baker Academic, 2005), 13.
[224] N. T Wright, *Simply Jesus: Who He Was, What He Did, Why It Matters* (London: SPCK, 2011), 180.
[225] Christine D. Pohl, *Making Room: Recovering Hospitality as a Christian Tradition* (Grand Rapids: W.B. Eerdmans, 1999), 30.
[226] S.S.Bartchy in Joel B Green (ed.), *Dictionary of Jesus and the Gospels* (Downers Grove: Intervarsity Press, 2013), 796–800.

The Applicatory Values of *Koinonia*

In Chapter 4, I concluded genuine *koinonia* has four enduring values: (1) a dynamic cruciform partnership; (2) an authentic and deep commitment; (3) generous and contributive participation; and (4) enduring circumstantial sharing. I contend that these values, evidenced in the early church (e.g. Ac.2:47), ideally summarise appropriate expectations for healthy participation, as described in Chapter 2. Family Table Ecclesiology mirrors *koinonia* values while simultaneously harbouring the potential to meet the needs of those whose lives reflect the values of postmodernity. Accordingly, these four principles of *koinonia* are central to Family Table Ecclesiology, through which *koinocovenantal commitment* can be expressed.

Koinonia Value 01: A Dynamic Cruciform Partnership

In all that has been said thus far, an apparent tension exists between being too assertive or too frightened to ask for a commitment. Leeman speaks about membership being a 'weighty' issue, arguing that the greatest tragedy of evangelicalism is an underdeveloped theology which conspires with prevailing individualistic societal attitudes against the 'one another' commitment advocated below. Consequently, he concludes, churches become shallow, weak and indistinguishable from the world.[227] In future, a repeated invitation and consistent teaching about *koinocovenantal commitment* will counter-culturally, yet thoroughly consistent with biblical values, promote an attitude of 'all of us and Jesus' not 'just me and Jesus.'

The ongoing promotion of the family sharing table metaphor is advantageous in overcoming individualism's

---

[227] Jonathan Leeman, *The Church and the Surprising Offense of God's Love*, 216–17.

hurdles since remaining at the family table without subscribing to its values, which promote participatory contribution(s) to honour God and others, is indefensible. Everyone is expected to participate as they are able, contributing to the cruciform conversation and sharing the same meal. Participation solidifies belonging and, consistent with the psychological theories outlined in Chapter 3, belonging and contributing something of value promotes ever-increasing commitment to mutually shared goals. Caution is required in application however, since commitment to Christ must be encouraged first; the error of conflating a person's commitment to the church with their commitment to Christ must be circumvented albeit, as argued, the two are not mutually exclusive.

Koinonia Value 02: An Authentic and Deep Commitment

As argued in Chapter 3, the pre-SAGA generation(s) do not satisfactorily find deep connection within perceived forms of institutionalised church. However, despite their anti-institution and anti-authority inclinations, they are not anti-community, especially if that community espouses values or promotes a cause which touches their emotions. Dulles, argues that one of the most significant failures of any church is to allow the institutional elements of corporate life to become its primary purpose, insomuch that rules and configuration of the machine become more important than people and their relationships.[228] Continuance with Restaurant Ecclesiology merits this accusation, whereas the promotion of Family Table Ecclesiology will overcome the hurdle. However, Leeman warns against excessive pendulum swings between the false dichotomy of love and structure, insightfully arguing for a 'both-and,' rather than 'either-or approach.' 'An over-emphasis in either direction

---

[228] Avery Dulles, *Models of the Church* (New York: Image Books, 2002), 27.

yields an image of something less than divine.'[229]

As argued in Chapter 2, such a utilitarian image is indefensible theologically. To avoid disfunction, healthy families incorporate structure, discipline and authority, but love must precede them. Any application of Family Table Ecclesiology must consider these factors. Peterson is right: 'The moment we begin to see others in terms of what they can *do* rather than who they *are*, we mutilate humanity and violate community.'[230]

Family Table Ecclesiology, like a functional biological family, simultaneously sustains love and structure in perfect tension.   Love, support, security and mutual encouragement enable personal spiritual growth. In its shadow, a diligently considered church structure provides a plasmatic framework for love to be appropriately expressed. The values and language of Family Table Ecclesiology are structured enough to give a robust framework; flexible enough to allow the Spirit to lead; encouraging enough to increase our commitment to Christ, and loose enough to help people belong at the beginning of their spiritual journey.

In sympathy with Hiebert's convictions, Family Table Ecclesiology 'make[s] people more important than programs, give[s] relationships priority over order and cleanliness,'[231] prioritising the needs of postmodern believers' despite their anti-authoritarian, anti-institutional inclinations without compromising the need for sound governance. Thus, leaders promoting Family Table

---

[229] Jonathan Leeman, *The Church and the Surprising Offense of God's Love*, 29.
[230] Eugene Peterson, *Working The Angles*, 71.
[231] Hiebert, *Anthropological Reflections on Missiological Issues*, 134.

Ecclesiology must diligently consider the prioritisation of relationships over excessive programming and/or governance.

Zizioulas argues that since God consists as a community of persons, humanity, made in the image of God, also craves to exist not as individuals but as community.[232] Not unlike the SAGA generation, this is especially true of the pre-SAGA generation(s) in our context. They are eager to be identified with the community, hence a willingness to initially come into Membership. With integrity, at the inception of membership commitment, the pre-SAGA generation(s) long to experience intimacy and participate, but, unconsciously, through the fog of postmodernist values and the complexity of life circumstances it propagates, deep connections allude them.

Burke contends, 'that to be effective, the emerging church must create a culture of connection. If the Boomer generation valued anonymity above all else when coming to church, the emerging [pre-SAGA] generations value connection above all else.'[233] I would further emphasise that this connection must be first to Christ, then to his Body. What Burke describes is that which was concluded in Chapter 1: the pre-SAGA generation(s) lack depth of connection despite their desire for it, and so instead content themselves with shallow ways of relating which is reflected in their commitment levels.[234] Authentic and deep *koinonia* connections within Family Table Ecclesiology are part of the solution as we move forwards.

---

[232] Jean Zizioulas, *Being as Communion: Studies in Personhood and the Church* (London: Darton Longman & Todd, 2004), 16-19, 36-65.
[233] John Burke, *No Perfect People Allowed: Creating a Come as You Are Culture in the Church.* (Grand Rapids: Zondervan, 2007), 268–69.
[234] John Burke, *No Perfect People Allowed,* 269–73.

Koinonia Value 03: Generous and Contributive Participation

Burke's argument is consistent with the psychological theories outlined in chapter 3: low participation promotes meagre commitment. McGravan's Social Identity Theory accentuates the extent to which an individual's sense of identity is conditioned by the groups to which they belong. These individuals are more likely to overcome postmodernity's sociological inhibitions if their perception of joining the local church is akin to joining a family rather than an impersonal hierarchically directed institutional machine. While this is not a fair caricature of governance in most local church contexts, the perception lingers under Restaurant Ecclesiology and must be confronted.[235] Furthermore, Social Learning Theory contends that commitment becomes increasingly generous if individuals feel their contribution is making a worthwhile addition. Family Table Ecclesiology promotes a family-like, rather than institutional-like affirmation of participative contributions which, when applied, will increase levels of commitment even in a sizeable numerical context. Consequently, the pre-SAGA generation(s) must be affirmed from the offset as valued members of the family and should be expected, by virtue of that family association, to make contributions appropriate to their st(age), circumstances and/or gifting.

In the future, subject to a critical mass of individuals perceiving and celebrating their place around a family table, Bandura's Social Learning Theory supports the idea that this perception will become attractional as others watch and subsequently follow their example. A fresh perception has

---

[235] The significance of leadership perception and modelling will be considered further below.

the potential of leading individuals to reside somewhere between Fitcher's 'nuclear member' and 'model member' typologies, especially since Fitcher's definitions are not dissimilar to reasonable familial expectations. Notwithstanding these psychological theories, the prevailing, pervasive, nature of postmodernity's sociological influence should not be understated in application and will require repeated challenge with the values of *koinonia*.

Crucially, future implementation of Family Table Ecclesiology must assume the roles of members and leaders are also family-like, upholding, in my context, a baptistic ecclesiology facilitating leaders to lead, serve *and* be served within a context where there is congregational ownership and execution. Within this model, gifting is affirmed, released and celebrated while recognising that we are part of a family within which every contribution is essential regardless of how menial or undesirable. Accordingly, leaders must have a mandate to lead while remaining accountable to Christ and the family.

Bandura's Social Learning Theory stresses the significance of leadership modelling, which is equally crucial within the family context. As I have written elsewhere, servant leadership (often misappropriated as 'slave leadership') is modelled using the metaphor of 'host leadership' which perfectly encapsulates value 03 of *koinonia*.[236] When applied, the 'host leadership' metaphor empowers leaders to seamlessly navigate the mutually conflicting requirements of leadership akin to the host of a family dinner-party who, skilfully, strategically and simultaneously,

---

[236] Chris Brockway, "Theological Theme: Servant Leadership" in *'M4: Developing Christian Leadership'* (Masters essay, Moorlands College, June 2018), 19-25.

is both leader and servant, perfectly circumnavigating preparation, attending, directing and co-participation. 'Host leadership is a way to [prominently] take a leading [initiating] position, in a way that [mutually] draws others in, in a natural [sacrificial yet assertive, co-defining] way.'[237]

Such an approach, in contrast to Restaurant Ecclesiology, is relational rather than transactional, while countenancing bespoke situational preferences needing to be addressed. Similarly, Lynch argues that such incarnational leadership, expressed as ecclesial leadership erring towards friendship, facilitates equality and participative service through personal vulnerability.[238] Poignantly, when Jesus superlatively modelled Family Table Ecclesiology while washing the disciples' feet, he was similarly acting as 'host' at the last-supper (John 13:1-17).

Koinonia Value 04: Enduring Circumstantial Sharing

For future application, having set the bar high for leaders and members alike with the preceding values of *koinonia*, this book challenges the inclination of many leaders to be cynically unsympathetic concerning the undulating reality of an individual's life circumstances. This needs to change moving forwards, since, as leaders, we must recognise we have more invested into the local church than it is reasonable to expect others to contribute, especially since the lives of members, especially those in the pre-SAGA generation(s), are demanding in ways which I cannot easily perceive. However, there must be a line drawn to ensure that members, whatever their situation, remain on the

---

[237] Mark McKergow and Helen L Bailey, *Host: Six New Roles of Engagement* (London: Solutions Books, 2014), 13.

[238] Chloe Lynch, *Ecclesial Leadership as Friendship*, Explorations in Practical, Pastoral, and Empirical Theology (New York: Routledge, 2019), 179–89.

'healthy side' of participation continuum which requires more than associated involvement.

As argued, Restaurant Ecclesiology's consumeristic mentality must be confronted. Within Family Table Ecclesiology application, a mutually affirmed *koinocovenantal commitment* (further explored below) must make the distinction between those who are 'unable' and those who are 'unwilling' to exercise participative commitment. Candidly stated, there is a marked difference between those who, through physical, emotional, relational or work-place challenges, are genuinely unable to commit horizontally, against those who are unwilling without a legitimate reason. The God-ward commitment must endure whatever the circumstance (e.g. Mt.24:13; Ro.5:3-4; 2 Tim.2:3, 4:5) since, as Paul affirms, *koinonia* does not cease because of hardship (Phil.3:10). In my experience, familial difficulties and suffering enable *koinonia* values to be more fully appreciated and tangibly perceived, which needs enduring comprehension. Family Table Ecclesiology promotes openness and sharing, which ought to make the challenges of individuals known, at least to the leadership, without the need for potentially inaccurate commitment assumptions being made.

Speaking about the privilege of church membership, Bonhoeffer wrote: 'Let him thank God on his knees and declare: it is grace, nothing but grace, that we are allowed to live in community with Christian brethren.' In all our theorising, if Family Table Ecclesiology has any value in application, one must not lose sight of the grace of God, which Bonhoeffer affirms. It is only by God's grace that we can belong, co-exist, contribute and participate.

The 'one another' commands of Scripture create a tension for Christians who are consciously or subconsciously living by postmodern individualistic and transient values. The 'one another' commands call for a medium to long-term view of relationships. One third of these commands concern church unity (Mk.9:50; Jn:6:43; Ro.12:6, 15:5, 15:7; 1 Cor.3:13, 11:33; Gal.5:15, 5:26; Eph.4:2, 4:32; 1 Thes.5:15; Ja.4:11, 5:9, 5:16); another third instruct believers to love one another (Jn.3:34, 15:12, 15:17, Ro.13:8; 1 Thes.3:12, 4:9; 1 Pe.1:22; 1 Jn.3:11, 4:7, 4:11, 2 Jn 5; Gal.5:13; Eph.4:2; 1 Pet.5:15; Ro.12:10); one sixth stress an attitude of humility and deference amongst believers (Jn.13:14; Ro.12:10, 12:16; Gal.5:13; Eph.5:21; Phil.2:3; 1 Pe.5:5); and the remaining sixth covers various other aspects of faith-filled living (Ro.14:13, 16:16; 1 Cor.3:9, 3:16, 7:5, 16:20; 2 Cor.13:12; Gal.6:2; Eph.4:25; 1 Thes.4:18, 5:11; Heb.10:24; Ja.5:16; 1 Pe.4:9).[239] Like any family, such relationships cannot be microwaved and demand longevity whatever the circumstances. Thus, Family Table Ecclesiology demands a long-term commitment from leaders and members alike.

Within the local church, there is no doubt that some people are more challenging to love than others. Consequently, like biological families, when applied, Family Table Ecclesiology will be difficult and disappointing. As affirmed above, sometimes life's circumstances conspire to prevent the kind of participation we might expect. Occasionally family relationships are inconvenient and demand enduring, even suffering, commitment. Family members sometimes make disagreeable and conflictual life choices requiring tenacity and forgiveness. While it might be right

---

[239] OverviewBible, 'All The "One Another" Commands in the NT' accessed July 15, 2019, https://overviewbible.com/one-another-infographic/

on occasions to move on, contrary to consumeristic Restaurant Ecclesiology, Family Table Ecclesiology calls for enduring love, whatever the situation, without thoughtless abandonment. Such values need persistent future promotion to counter expedient disloyalty, which is a consumeristic symptom of Restaurant Ecclesiology, but must not be part of the culture of Family Table Ecclesiology. Instead, "You matter, and we will not give up on you, even when you fail" ought to be the ongoing defining characteristic of Family Table Ecclesiology (FTE) and this final *koinonia* value. As Burke argues, covenantal families should 'interconnect like the strands of a net that only together have the strength to catch people in the free-fall of aloneness.'[240]

Koinocovenantal Commitment Combined With FTE

As elucidated in Chapter 2, formalised covenant agreements have been outmoded, especially within Baptist churches. Consequently, very few working examples can be found within progressive local churches. The finest, systematically and theologically considered examples, each of which, having experienced similar symptoms to Restaurant Ecclesiology, transitioned from membership affirmed by interview and congregational vote to membership corroborated via publicly signed covenant agreement. Echoing the principles described in Chapter 2, in summary, the covenant of such local churches tend to include the following:

- Confirmation of regenerate, continuing, faith in Christ
- Affirmation of commitment to the local church family

---

[240] John Burke, *No Perfect People Allowed*, 290.

- Pro-active engagement with spiritual disciplines
- Mutual accountability with and dependence upon other covenanted believers
- Submission to correction and discipline within the church
- A commitment to exercise natural, spiritual and grace gifts for ministry and mission

Such covenants clearly prioritise my aspirant three-fold trajectory described in Chapter 1. The postmodernist characteristics typical of the pre-SAGA generation(s) are robustly challenged since the covenant is shaped around Family Table Ecclesiology's participative values, not Restaurant Ecclesiology's consumeristic orientation. Familial language, calling for deep connection with God and thereafter the household of God will be attractive in meeting the felt needs of both the SAGA and especially pre-SAGA generation(s). Such a covenant promotes high expectations of members, however, like the early church and early Baptists (albeit not under circumstances of persecution), candidates will then exercise circumspect consideration at the point of candidacy or reaffirmation. Any use of such a covenant would require the founding commitment and any subsequent declaration to be consciously established upon the continuum between 'model' and 'nuclear' membership; a 'communal' rather than 'associative' commitment; thus, encouraging appraisal of the 'doctrinal orthodoxy' and 'devotionalism' measurements as summarised in Chapter 3.

Significantly, any such covenant must be purposefully appended to a local church's ethos, core value and values statement. Therefore, commitment to the latter is presupposed of the former and vice versa, which is prudent since a church's ethos and values significantly influence the prevailing identity of the community to which the covenant is being made.

My contention is that the example covenant above constitutes an exemplary template for *koinocovenantal commitment*, to support *koinocovenant commitment* and Family Table Ecclesiology. Like the example covenant, it would be publicly affirmed, annually confirmed and, at least on the first occasion, signed before the whole congregation. In the light of the findings of this book thus far however, I propose additionally appending the church's constitution (where applicable) and defining the role of leadership using the 'host' metaphor. Furthermore, *koinocovenantal commitment* would be clearly defined by wrapping it around the four principles of *koinonia* highlighted above, while unambiguously advancing examples of various ways that each value might be tangibly expressed. The above would need to be documented and unashamedly communicated using the biblical and theologically poignant familial language of Family Table Ecclesiology.

At least one final challenge remains in the application of FTE: as a church leader, I cannot make *koinocovenantal commitments* on behalf of others, but I can teach the necessity of integrity, the maintaining of commitments made and essential nature of a depth of connection which transcends being alone together in agreeable abandon. As stated in Chapter 2, to overcome the pre-SAGA generation(s) inhibitions regarding authority, local church leadership must remain thoroughly committed to modelling the values of Family Table Ecclesiology so that our aspirations will become our operant reality. Family must be prioritised ahead of institution.

Crucially in application, *koinocovenantal commitment* and Family Table Ecclesiology must not become controlling or coercive tools but rather a plasmatic framework affirming the value of each individual in Christ and in the Body. We should not expect too much and yet not expect too little. *Koinocovenantal commitment* is not a creed spelling out the church's understanding of particular doctrines; rather, it is a mutually agreed statement of intent, for every generation, SAGA or pre-SAGA, to relate to God and to 'one another,' as deeply committed and connected disciples, around the metaphorical table of Family Table Ecclesiology.

Conclusion

The problem of Restaurant Ecclesiology was described in chapter 1. This model was evaluated to be an ineffectual and impoverished form of church, especially when compared to the early church described in Acts 2. The particular contribution the pre-SAGA (<50s) generation(s) make to this caricatured ecclesiological model were compared and contrasted with the SAGA (>50s) generation. My conclusion is that the latter are more committed (God-ward and undoubtedly other-ward) Members than the former.

Chapter 2 contrasted our contemporary experience with biblical, theological and historical principles for church membership. 'Membership' was argued to be implicit rather than explicit throughout the New Testament. I concluded that some form of membership in the contemporary church is necessary, even if only for pragmatic reasons, but especially for mutual accountability, developing mission and ministry, and sound congregational governance.

Various socio-psychological perspectives, particularly the impact of postmodernism upon the pre-SAGA generation(s), were evaluated in chapter 3. The primary sociological symptoms of postmodernism and its negative influence upon commitment levels were accentuated alongside various psychological considerations which contribute to reduced commitment amongst the pre-SAGA generation(s). I concluded, however, that questions of a theological nature ought to transcend socio-psychological axioms as they relate to participative church membership commitment. Whilst separating belief from belonging to authenticate sociological phenomena might be expedient, this is never appropriate from a theological perspective. Thomas argues that belief is in itself 'the most potent form of belonging'[241] and yet the idea that 'belonging somehow authenticates belief [or commitment] is theologically inadequate.'[242] I concur.

In chapter 4, consideration was given to the historical significance and ongoing contemporary value of covenants to both express and cultivate commitment in the 'visible' church. It was concluded that traditional concepts of covenant, encompassing mutually accountable, cruciform, discipleship relationships, foundational to Scripture and particularly Baptist ecclesiology, must be rediscovered and reframed through the coining of a new phrase in local church contexts: *koinocovenant(al) commitment*.

---

[241] Richard Thomas, *Counting People In: Changing the Way We Think about Membership and the Church* (London: SPCK, 2003), v.
[242] Richard Thomas, *Counting People In*, v.

In chapter 5, the application of a replacement ecclesiological metaphor for Restaurant Ecclesiology was advocated, Family Table Ecclesiology, within which *koinocovenantal commitment* (which necessitates a publicly corroborated affirmation), can be both encouraged and efficaciously expressed, seeking to confront the postmodern challenges associated with the pre-SAGA generation(s). It is envisaged that the new, Family Table Ecclesiology, metaphor will transcend mere academic comprehension of the issues, instead becoming a sharp(er) tool to change the way we think about our ecclesiology at an unconscious level.

If, as my local church's 'Introduction to Membership' booklet contends, and as Leeman argues, 'joining a church is a momentous and awesome thing,'[243] the bar of Membership needs to be raised beyond a solemn handshake, rather (re)affirming and making visible our pre-existing adoption into the family of God and the decision to change allegiances from Satan to God. This is not only primarily an individual Godward covenant but equally a reminder for all who have taken this path before that they too should celebrate their own identification with this journey as part of the same family, regardless of which side of the 'SAGA' divide they find themselves.

Family Table Ecclesiology, which expresses *koinocovenantal commitment*, could prove a meaningful way, even if only partially, of resolving the Church Membership SAGA.

---

[243] Jonathan Leeman, *The Church and the Surprising Offense of God's Love*, 252.

Appendix A | Summary of Covenants In The Old Testament

Old Testament covenants and a summary of their significance are listed below in chronological order.

The Edenic and Adamic Covenants (Genesis 1:26-28 & 3:14-19)

The Bible begins with God's conditional Edenic (pre-fall) Covenant[244] over creation, which is expressed to Adam (Gen.1:26-30; 2:16-17), as 'the covenant head of the human race.'[245] At the heart of this agreement is God's command not to eat from the tree of the knowledge of good and evil (Ge.2:16-17). Adam (and Eve) failed to obey the terms of this covenant and suffered the prescribed consequences of physical and spiritual death and lifelong gruelling labour (Gen.4:17-19). From the first days of creation, to maintain any relationship with God, it is evident that fallen humanity would require his grace which is expressed through the succeeding Adamic (post-fall)

---

[244] This covenant is sometimes referred to as 'Covenant of Works.' Although not described as a covenant in Genesis, Hosea later referred to it as such (Hos.6:7).
[245] Peter John Gentry and Stephen J. Wellum, *God's Kingdom through God's Covenants*, 612.

Covenant (Gen.3:14-24).[246] The Adamic Covenant is the first grace orientated promise found in the Scriptures concerning redemption and the protoevangelium:[247] 'I will put enmity between you and the woman, and between your offspring and hers; he [Satan] will crush your head, and you will strike his heel.' (Ge.3:15). In combination, these first two covenants reveal that sin has consequences, resulting in a spiralling sin-judgement-grace pattern, repeated throughout Scripture but ultimately reconciled in Christ. The Edenic and Adamic covenants, communicated to Adam as representative of all humanity (Ro.5:12; 1 Cor.15:22), sets the stage for the age, revealing God's intention for his creation to glorify him righteously, an intention he returns to at the end of the age (Rev.21-22).

The Noahic Covenant (Genesis 8:20-9:6)

God's renewed commitment to humanity, expressed through Noah, is significant since it is the first time the word 'covenant' is explicitly used to define the relational agreement established (Ge.6:18). The covenantal "if" necessitated obedience/trust in building the ark and God's "then, I will" pledges enduring worldwide flood-protection (Ge.9:9-17). The outworking of the covenant is unconditional, requiring nothing of Noah, other than his initial obedience to fulfil the covenant. Weinfield, therefore, understands this to be a covenant in the form of 'a grant' since God alone is obligated to keep its tenets.[248] Through the sign of the rainbow (Ge.9:12-13), God's covenantal purpose is to remind humanity of his

---

[246] Like the Edenic Covenant, this covenant is not explicitly described as a covenant in Genesis but is nonetheless a significant promise made in response to The Fall.
[247] The first announcement of the Gospel in Scripture.
[248] Moshe Weinfield in "The Covenant of Grant in the Old Testament and in the Ancient Near East," *Journal of the American Oriental Society,* 90 (1970), 185.

unsurpassed holiness and grace-filled faithfulness. Consistent with the sin-judgement-grace spiral mentioned above, humanity rebels at Babel, God scatters people into ethnic groups (Gen.11:1-9), and the succeeding covenant, the Abrahamic Covenant, is established as a supplementary expression of God's enduring grace.

The Abrahamic Covenant (Genesis 12:1-3)

God initiates a renewed pilgrimage around the sin-judgement-grace spiral with a new covenantal promise (Ge.12:1-3) to make Abraham a great nation, ceremoniously formalised (Gen.15:9-11) and symbolised through circumcision (Gen.17:9-14). This covenant has been described as the greatest of redemptive covenants,[249] foundational to OT theology, since it becomes the proximate cause for all of God's successive blessings, first to a specific people, the Jews, and then to the Gentiles (Gen.12:1-37, 13:14-17; 15:1-21; 17:1-21; 22:15-18).[250] Significantly, fulfilment of this covenant is unconditional (there are no "ifs"); literal (i.e. specific land is promised, Ge.12:1, 13:14-18, 15:18-21; Deut.30:1-10; cf. Jos.21:43); and, everlasting (God's promise to Israel is eternal). The Abrahamic Covenant is subsequently fulfilled and expanded in the form of the following three sub-covenants: (1) the Mosaic Covenant; (2) the Davidic Covenant; and (3) the New Covenant (NC).

The Mosaic Covenant (Exodus 20:1-31:18)

At Sinai, as God recalled his unilateral Abrahamic Covenant. Moses was the next leader elected to mediate a bilateral,

---

[249] Jeong Koo Jeon, *Biblical Theology: Covenants and the Kingdom of God in Redemptive History* (Eugene: Wipf & Stock, 2017), 220–21.
[250] Peter John Gentry and Stephen J. Wellum, *God's Kingdom through God's Covenants*, 259-261.

conditional, covenant with Israel (Ex.20:1-31:18). Through Abraham, God had formed a people (Ex.4:22; Deut.8:5) and through Moses, to rescue his people from bondage, God establishes a national constitution for effective witness (e.g. Deut.4:5-6; Ex.19:6; Ps.22:25-28; 1 Chr.16:8; Jer.4:1) and recognition of sin (2 Cor.3:7-9). This defined people would be 'the agent used by God to achieve the wider purposes which the Abrahamic covenant entails.'[251]

The Mosaic Covenant detailed expected spiritual, ethical and ritual laws which exemplify God's holiness (Ex.9:13-16, 34:10-16; Deut.7:6-9, 26:16-19; Isa.63:11-14; Lev.11:44).[252] These laws were not evidence of a legalistic relationship, but rather an expression of God's grace to facilitate the experience of life in its fullness: 'covenants do not produce relationships, they affirm a relationship which already exists and give further structure to those relationships.'[253]

While the Mosaic Covenant has continuity with the Abrahamic Covenant, as Dumbrell emphasises, it is both purposeful (to be an identifiable people) and conditional ("if you obey my voice").[254] Moreover, this agreement is conditional upon humanities response to God's commands (Ex.19:5-6). The Mosaic Covenant continues the progressive accentuation of God's holiness and defines the parameters (Ro.3:20; cf. Ex.20:1-17; Deut.5:6-21) within which that holiness should be reflected in his people (Deut.6:5; Lev.19:2,18; Mt.22:36-40; 1 Pe.1:16).

---

[251] W. J Dumbrell, *Covenant and Creation: A Theology of the Old Testament Covenants.* (Carlisle: Paternoster, 2000), 89.

[252] Stephen G. Dempster, *Dominion and Dynasty: A Biblical Theology of the Hebrew Bible*, New Studies in Biblical Theology 15 (Leicester: Apollos, 2003), 172–74.

[253] T. Desmond Alexander, *From Paradise to the Promised Land: An Introduction to the Pentateuch* (Grand Rapids: Baker Academic, 2012), 166.

[254] W.J Dumbrell, *Covenant and Creation*, 89.

The Davidic Covenant (2 Samuel 7:4-17)

The Davidic Covenant (2 Sam.7; summarised in 1 Chr.17:11-14 and 2 Chr.6:16), is part of the evolving story which has continuity with the preceding covenants, providing, as Dumbrell, Gentry and Wellum argue, further clarity to the Mosaic Covenant while moving the Abrahamic Covenant closer to fulfilment in Christ:[255] 'The Davidic king becomes the mediator of covenant blessing, tied back to Abraham, ultimately tied back to Adam.'[256] The Davidic Covenant is lateral, unconditional and its promises are eternal: most significantly God promises that the Messiah would come from the lineage of David, a promise cross-referenced throughout the Scriptures (e.g. Jer.23:5, 30:9; Isa.9:7,11:1; Lk.1:32, 69; Ac.13:34; Rev.3:7, etc.).

---

[255] W.J.Dumbrell, *Covenant and Creation*, 127, 150-152.
[256] Peter John Gentry and Stephen J. Wellum, *God's Kingdom through God's Covenants*, 702.

Appendix B | Etymological Methodology For 'Koinocovenantal Commitment'

The words 'covenant' and 'commitment' each start with the same Latin prefix 'cum' meaning 'with.' When used as a prefix, it takes the form 'com-' or 'co-' depending on the first letter of the component to which it is joined.[257] This rule is applied to 'covenant' and 'commitment' by changing the 'm' to the letter it precedes; other examples include 'connect', 'correct', 'collude.'

'Mens' is a Latin word meaning 'mind,' 'understanding,' 'idea.'[258] The 's' in 'mens' is changed to 't' when it becomes a suffix (i.e. '-ment') or has suffixes added to it.[259] So adding the suffix '-ment' is one way of shifting the function of a noun to a verb: 'commit.'[260] Two other nouns made from 'commit' are 'committal'[261] and 'commission,'[262] both of

---

[257] https://www.vocabulary.com/lists/284889 accessed June 30, 2019.
[258] https://latin-dictionary.net/search/latin/mens accessed June 30, 2019.
[259] https://www.etymonline.com/word/-ment accessed June 30, 2019.
[260] https://www.etymonline.com/search?q=commitment accessed June 30, 2019.
[261] https://www.etymonline.com/search?q=commital accessed June 30, 2019.
[262] https://www.etymonline.com/search?q=commission accessed 30 June 2019.

which are illuminating words considering our theme. The central component of these words comes from the Latin word 'mitto' meaning 'I send'[263] (again, the 't' changes to an 's' in some tenses of the verb and when linking it with different suffixes).

The etymology of 'covenant' is 'Latin: con-; venire, to come.' 'Ven' is the component which means 'come'; '-ire' is the suffix making it the infinitive verb 'to come.' Consequently, the etymology can be read literally as 'to come with' or 'to come together with'[264] or 'agreeing' from the Old French.[265] The suffix '-ant' in Old French is based on the Latin suffix which turns the verb for 'agree' into the noun for the process of 'agreeing' or for the statement which results from 'agreeing.'[266]

So, following McKean's principles for pioneering new words, my new word/phrase would be most apparent if all the letters of the components that are needed to express the meaning I am seeking to convey could be included recognisably in my new word. For example, the following words could be considered:

- 'Covement' – although it arguably conveys the concept of things enclosed literally or metaphorically in a cove (small rocky bay; or arch where a wall meets a ceiling).
- 'Covenment' – but it might unhelpfully convey association with people in a coven (e.g. a gathering of witches).
- 'Comcovment' - has the prefix 'com-' and the suffix

---

[263] http://www.latin-dictionary.net/search/latin/mitto accessed June 30, 2019.
[264] https://www.etymonline.com/search?q=covenant accessed June 30, 2019.
[265] https://www.lexico.com/en/definition/covenant accessed June 30, 2019.
[266] https://www.etymonline.com/search?q=agreement accessed 30 June 2019

'-ment' but would not be evident to the reader that 'cov' comes from 'covenant.'
- 'Comovement' – is a word which already exists, meaning 'correlated or similar movement of two or more entities.'[267] Since this is not a new word, I will avoid using it, although, given its definition, it would suggest my attempts are headed in the correct direction.

Significantly, the prefix 'com-' has some historic influence from the Classical Greek word 'koinonia' meaning 'fellowship,' a transliteration of the Greek word (κοινωνία) meaning communion.[268] 'Koinonia' depicts a joint participative cruciform relationship, vertically and horizontally, between God and believers who are sharing new life through Christ.[269] 'Koinonia' captures the entirety of this relationship (e.g. Ac.2:42; 2 Cor.9:13; Phil.3:10). Since the historical cruciform nature of church membership has repeatedly been accentuated throughout this essay, it would seem very appropriate to include all or part of the word 'koinonia' or its root word 'koinos' in my new word/phrase to emphasise the God-ward and other-ward nature of membership.

John uses *koinonia* to describe the sense of 'partnership' which connects believers to God and each other in Christ (1 Jn.1:9). In continuity with his Gospel, Luke uses *koinonia* to describe the 'fellowship' of the early church (Ac.2:42), observing an authentic and deep commitment which was more than a mere informal social gathering (which is frequently how 'fellowship' is insouciantly considered in the

---

[267] https://www.yourdictionary.com/comovement accessed 30 June 2019
[268] Strong, *Strong's Exhaustive Concordance of the Bible*, G2842.
[269] Strong, *Strong's Exhaustive Concordance of the Bible*, G2842.

contemporary church). Paul uses the word *koinonia* in 2 Corinthians 9:13 to affirm participation in a generous 'contribution' and then in Philippians 3:10 to speak of 'sharing' in the suffering of Christ. The values of *koinonia* outlined above, only made possible by renewal and regenerate faith in Christ (e.g. Eph.4:23; Ro.12:2; 2 Cor.4:16; Col.3:10; Tit.3: 5), stand in stark contrast to the values of postmodernity which, as discussed, broadly speaking reflect the values of our pre-SAGA generation(s). In summary of these different uses of *koinonia*, we can say that genuine *koinonia* is: (1) a dynamic cruciform (God-ward and other-ward) partnership; (2) an authentic and deep commitment; (3) generous and contributive participation; and (4) enduring circumstantial sharing. See Chapter 5.

'Koinocovenant' or 'koinonicovenant' could be used to indicate that Christian commitment draws from both the OT emphasis on covenants and the NT emphasis on fellowship/communion/sharing relationships. Creating such a word as a noun might appear to need a fixed set of commitments as a definition, so it could be distinctly used as an adjective, made evident by adding the suffix '-al': e.g. 'koinocovenantal commitment' or 'koinonicovenantal commitment') to indicate that Christian commitment blends elements from both those traditions. 'Koinonicovenantal' more clearly comes from 'koinonia,' but 'koinocovenantal' might be easier to say and consequently more memorable.

In Greek, 'koinos' means 'common' in the general sense (e.g. Ac.2:44 and 4:32), but also 'common' in the sense of 'unclean' (e.g. Mk 7:2,5, Ac.10:14, 28, 11:8).[270] Arguably, a tiny minority with Greek knowledge might make the

---

[270] Strong, *Strong's Exhaustive Concordance of the Bible*, G2839.

association with 'unclean' but since 'koinos' has not become a common word in Christian discussion like 'koinonia' has, the vast majority would accept and recognise the word 'koinocovenantal' as meaning 'drawing from the traditions of both koinonia and covenant.' For 'koinocovenant' or 'koinocovenantal' to be understood as coming from 'koinonia,' the second 'o' should be pronounced as in the word 'hotel,' not as in 'hot', because 'koinonia' (κοινωνια) has the Greek letter omega ω, not omicron o as in 'koinos' (κοινος).[271]

---

[271] Compare pronunciation in Strong, *Strong's Exhaustive Concordance of the Bible*, G2842; Strong, *Strong's Exhaustive Concordance of the Bible*, G2839.

Bibliography

Abrams, Dominic. *Social Identifications: A Social Psychology of Intergroup Relations and Group Processes*. New York: Routledge, 2016.

Adams, J. Michael, and Angelo Carfagna. *Coming of Age in a Globalized World: The next Generation*. Bloomfield: Kumarian Press, 2006.

Agger, Ben. *A Critical Theory Of Public Life: Knowledge, Discourse And Politics In An Age Of Decline.* Hoboken: Taylor and Francis, 2013.

Alexander, Jeffrey C, and Kenneth Thompson. *A Contemporary Introduction to Sociology: Culture and Society in Transition*. Boulder: Paradigm Publishers, 2008.

Alexander, T. Desmond. *From Paradise to the Promised Land: An Introduction to the Pentateuch*. Grand Rapids: Baker Academic, 2012.

Appignanesi, Richard, Chris Garratt, Ziauddin Sardar, and Patrick Curry. *Introducing Postmodernism*. New York: Totem Books, 1995.

Arnold, Clinton E. *Power and Magic: The Concept of Power in Ephesians*. Cambridge: Cambridge University Press, 1989.

Balz, Horz, and Gerhard Schneider. *Exegetical Dictionary of the New Testament,* Vol. 1. 3 vols. Grand Rapids: Eerdmans, 1990.

Bandura, Albert. *Social Learning Theory*. Englewood Cliffs: Prentice Hall, 1977.

Baptist Union of Great Britain (The). *Article 1 of the Declaration of Principle,* accessed July 09, 2019, www.baptist.org.uk/Publisher/File.aspx?ID=216696.

———. Covenant 21: Covenant for a Gospel People. The Baptist Union: Didcot, 2001.

Barth, Karl, G. W Bromiley, and Thomas F Torrance. *Church Dogmatics. Volume IV, Part 2, Volume IV, Part 2,*. Edinburgh: Bloomsbury Publishing, 2000. http://public.eblib.com/choice/publicfullrecord.aspx?p=1748860.

Bauman, Zygmunt. *Liquid Modernity*. Cambridge: Polity Press, 2000.

BBC News. 'National Trust membership hits new high of five million.' 23 September 2017, accessed July 09, 2019, https://www.bbc.co.uk/news/uk-41361095.

———. 'Saving Pounds: the rise of the budget gym.' 16 July 2018, accessed July 09, 2019, https://www.bbc.co.uk/news/business-44766250.

Beaumont, Kate, Donna Cobban, Belinda Train, and Julie Wellman. *Introduction to Psychology*. Cape Town: Pearson Prentice Hall, 2007.

Bebbington, David William. *Evangelicalism in Modern Britain: A History from the 1730s to the 1980s*. London: Unwin & Hyman, 1995.

Beck, Ulrich, and Elisabeth Beck-Gernsheim. *Individualization: Institutionalized Individualism and Its Social and Political Consequences*. Theory, Culture & Society. London: SAGE, 2002.

Ben Agger State University of New York, Buffalo, USA. *A Critical Theory Of Public Life: Knowledge, Discourse And Politics In An Age Of Decline*. Hoboken: Taylor and Francis, 2013. http://www.123library.org/book_details/?id=113599.

Berger, Peter L. "Secularism in Retreat." *The National Interest*. December 01, 1996.

———. *The Heretical Imperative: Contemporary Possibilities of Religious Affirmation*. Garden City: Anchor Press, 1980.

Berger, Peter, and Anton Zijderveld. *In Praise of Doubt: How to Have Convictions Without Becoming a Fanatic*. New York: HarperOne, 2014.

Berman, Marshall. *All That Is Solid Melts into Air: The Experience of Modernity*. London: Verso, 2010.

Blyth, M (ed.). *Joined-up Thinking: Membership*. Didcot: The Baptist Union of Great Britain, 2004.

Bray, Gerald Lewis. *The Church: A Theological and Historical Account*. Grand Rapids: Baker Academic, 2016.

Brockway, Chris. "Theological Theme: Servant Leadership" in *'M4: Developing Christian Leadership'*. Masters essay, Moorlands College, June 2018.

Brown, Callum G. *Postmodernism for Historians*. Harlow: Pearson, 2005.

Brown, Rupert. *Group Processes: Dynamics within and between Groups*. 2nd ed. Oxford, UK ; Malden, Mass: Blackwell Publishers, 2001.

Burke, John. *No Perfect People Allowed: Creating a Come as You Are Culture in the Church*. Grand Rapids: Zondervan, 2007.

Call, Lewis. *Postmodern Anarchism*. Lanham: Lexington Books, 2002.

Campbell, A. 'The Grounds of Association' in A Perspective on Baptist Identity Kingsbridge: Mainstream, 1987.

Chandler, David, and William B. Werther. *Strategic Corporate Social Responsibility: Sustainable Value Creation*. Fourth edition. Los Angeles: SAGE, 2017.

Chester, Tim, and Steve Timmis. *Total Church: A Radical Reshaping around Gospel and Community*. Nottingham: Inter-Varsity Press, 2010.

Church of England, ed. *Common Worship: Services and Prayers for the Church of England*. London: Church House Publishing, 2000.

Clarke, A (ed.). "Baptists in Covenant" in Bound for Glory? God, Church and World in Covenant. Oxford: Whitley Publications, 2002.

Collyer, Michael. 'What Church For The SAGA Generation? Cultural shifts in the younger old,' Church Army: *"Discovering Faith in Later Life,"* issue 6, March 2007.

———. 'What Church For The SAGA Generation? Cultural Shifts in the Younger Old,' *Crucible: The Journal of Social Ethics*, April-June 2008.

Cools, Marc (ed). *Safety, Societal Problems and Citizen's Perceptions: New Empirical Data, Theories and Analyses*. Governance of Security Research Paper Series. Antwerpen: Maklu, 2010.

Colson, Chuck and Larson, Catherine. 'The Lost Art Of Commitment', *Christianity Today*, 04 August 2010, https://www.christianitytoday.com/ct/2010/august/10.49.html.

Covey, Stephen R., A. Roger Merrill, and Rebecca R. Merrill. *First Things First: To Live, to Love, to Learn, to Leave a Legacy*. New York: Free Press, 2003.

Church of England, ed., *Common Worship: Services and Prayers for the Church of England*. London: Church House Publ, 2000.

Cross, Frank Moore. *From Epic to Canon: History and Literature in Ancient Israel*. Johns Hopkins. A Johns Hopkins Paperback. Baltimore: The Johns Hopkins Univ. Press, 2000.

Crowther, Gillian. *Eating Culture: An Anthropological Guide to Food*. Toronto: University of Toronto Press, 2018.

Davie, Grace. *Religion in Britain since 1945: Believing without Belonging*. Making Contemporary Britain. Oxford ; Cambridge, Mass: Blackwell, 1994.

———. *The Sociology of Religion: A Critical Agenda*. Second edition. Los Angeles: SAGE, 2013.

Dempster, Stephen G. *Dominion and Dynasty: A Biblical Theology of the Hebrew Bible*. New Studies in Biblical Theology 15. Leicester: Apollos, 2003.

Dever, Mark. *A Display of God's Glory: Basics of Church Structure : Deacons, Elders, Congregationalism & Membership*. Washington: 9Marks, 2010.

Dever, Mark, and Paul Alexander. *The Deliberate Church: Building Your Ministry on the Gospel*. Wheaton: Crossway Books, 2005.

Dever, Mark, Jonathan Leeman, and James Leo Garrett. *Baptist Foundations: Church Government for an Anti-Institutional Age*. Nashville: B&H Publishing Group, 2015. **http://public.eblib.com/choice/publicfullrecord.aspx?p=3563382**.

Dulles, Avery. *Models of the Church*. New York: Image Books, 2002.

Dumbrell, W. J. *Covenant and Creation: A Theology of the Old Testament Covenants*. Carlisle: Paternoster, 2000.

Engelsviken, Tormod, Erling Lundeby, and Dagfinn Solheim, eds. *The Church Going Glocal: Mission and Globalisation ; [Proceedings of the Fjellhaug Symposium 2010]*. Regnum Edinburgh 2010 Series. Oxford: Regnum, 2011.

Estep, William Roscoe. *The Anabaptist Story: An Introduction to Sixteenth-Century Anabaptism*. Grand Rapids: William B. Eerdmans Pub, 1996.

Ferguson, Sinclair B. *The Holy Spirit*. Leicester: I.V.P. United Kingdom, 1996.

Feucht, Oscar E. *Everyone a Minister: A Guide to Churchmanship for Laity and Clergy*. St. Louis: Concordia Pub. House, 1994.

Fichter, Joseph Henry. *Social Relations in the Urban Parish*. Chicago: Chicago University Press, 1954.

Fiddes, Paul S. *The Nature of the Assembly and the Council of the Baptist Union of Great Britain*. Didcot: The Baptist Union of Great Britain, 1994.

———. *Tracks and Traces: Baptist Identity in Church and Theology*. Studies in Baptist History and Thought 13. Eugene, OR: Wipf and Stock, 2006.

Fiddes, P.S; Hayden, R; Kidd, R.L; et al. (eds.), *Bound to Love: the Covenant Basis of Baptist Life and Mission*. London: The Baptist Union, 1985.

Fiddes, P.S; Haymes, B; Kidd, B; et al. (eds.) 'Theology and a Baptist Way of Community' in *Doing Theology in a Baptist Way*. Oxford: Whitley Publications, 2000.

Forrester, Duncan B., William Storrar, and Andrew Morton, eds. *Public Theology for the 21st Century: Essays in Honour of Duncan B. Forrester*. London: T&T Clark, 2004.

Forsyth, Donelson R. *Group Dynamics*. Boston: Cengage, 2019.

Frey, Dave; Glover, Ben; McDonald, Ben, *Come to the Table,* Warner/Chappell Music, Inc, Capitol Christian Music Group, Universal Music Publishing Group.

Fuchs, Lorelei F. *Koinonia and the Quest for an Ecumenical Ecclesiology: From Foundations through Dialogue to Symbolic Competence for Communionality*. Grand Rapids: William B. Eerdmans Pub. Co, 2008.

Garrett, James Leo. *Baptist Theology: A Four-Century Study*. Macon: Mercer University Press, 2009.

Gentry, Peter John, and Stephen J. Wellum. *God's Kingdom through God's Covenants: A Concise Biblical Theology*. Wheaton: Crossway, 2015.

Gibbs, Eddie, and Ian Coffey. *Church next: Quantum Changes in How We Do Ministry*. Leicester: Inter-Varsity Press, 2001.

Gibney, Bruce Cannon. *A Generation of Sociopaths: How the Baby Boomers Betrayed America*. First edition. New York: Hachette Books, 2017.

Giddens, Anthony, ed. *Social Theory Today*. Cambridge: Polity Press, 1993.

Giddens, Anthony, and Christopher Pierson. *Conversations with Anthony Giddens: Making Sense of Modernity*. Stanford: Stanford University Press, 1998.

Gilmore, A. *The Pattern of the Church: A Baptist View*. London: Lutterworth Press, 1963.

Glueck, Nelson. *Hesed in the Bible*. Eugene: Wipf & Stock Publishers, 2011.

Green, Francis; Felstead, Alan; Gallie, Duncan and Henseke, Golo. 'Work Intensity in Britain: First Findings from the Skills and Employment Survey

2017.' Cardiff: Cardiff University, 2017, accessed June 25, 2019, https://www.cardiff.ac.uk/__data/assets/pdf_file/0009/1309455/4_Intensity_Minireport_Final.pdf

Green, Joel B. *Dictionary of Jesus and the Gospels*. Downers Grove: Intervarsity Press, 2013.

Green, Lynn. "Renewing The Covenant," *Baptists Together: the magazine for the Baptist Union of Great Britain*. Spring 2016.

Grenz, Stanley J., and John R. Franke. *Beyond Foundationalism: Shaping Theology in a Postmodern Context*. Louisville: Westminster John Knox Press, 2001.

Guder, Darrell L., and Lois Barrett, eds. *Missional Church: A Vision for the Sending of the Church in North America*. The Gospel and Our Culture Series. Grand Rapids: W.B. Eerdmans Pub, 1998.

Gushee, David P. *In the Fray: Contesting Christian Public Ethics, 1994-2013*. Eugene: Cascade Books, 2014.

Guttal, Shalmali. *Globalisation: Development in Practice*, accessed October 11, 2019, www.jstor.org/stable/25548249.

Hahn, Scott. *Kinship by Covenant: A Canonical Approach to the Fulfillment of God's Saving Promises*. The Anchor Yale Bible Reference Library. New Haven: Yale University Press, 2009.

Hammett, John S. *Biblical Foundations for Baptist Churches: A Contemporary Ecclesiology*. Grand Rapids: Kregel Publications, 2005.

Hanson, Amy. *Baby Boomers and beyond: Tapping the Ministry Talents and Passions of Adults over Fifty*. Leadership Network. San Francisco: Jossey-Bass, 2010.

Haykin, Michael, A.G. 'The Baptist Identity: A View From the Eighteenth Century', *The Evangelical Quarterly*, EQ67:2, 1995.

Haymes, B. "On Being the Church" in A Call to Mind: Baptist Essays towards a theology of Commitment. London: The Baptist Union of Great Britain, 1981.

Healy, Nicholas M. *Church, World, and the Christian Life: Practical-Prophetic Ecclesiology*. Cambridge Studies in Christian Doctrine. Cambridge: Cambridge University Press, 2000.

Hiebert, Paul G. *Anthropological Reflections on Missiological Issues*. Grand Rapids: Baker Books, 1994.

Hugenberger, Gordon P. *Marriage as a Covenant: Biblical Law and Ethics as Developed from Malachi*. Eugene: Wipf & Stock, 2014.

Hunter, George G. *Church for the Unchurched*. Nashville: Abingdon Press, 1996.

Huntington, Samuel P., and Francis Fukuyama. *Political Order in Changing Societies*. New Haven: Yale Univ. Press, 2006.

Huyssen, Andreas. *After the Great Divide: Modernism, Mass Culture, Postmodernism*. New York: ACLS Humanities E-Book.

Jackson, Darrell Richard. "The Covenantal Discourse of Contemporary Baptist Belonging and Membership," in *The Discourse of 'Belonging' and Baptist Church Membership In Contemporary Britain: Historical, Theological and Demotic Elements of a Post-Foundational Theological Proposal*. Birmingham: University of Birmingham, 2009.

James, Paul. *Making Modernity from the Mashriq to the Maghreb*, "They Have Never Been Modern? Then

What Is the Problem with Those Persians?". Melbourne: Arena Publications, 2015.

Jamieson, Bobby. *Going Public: Why Baptism Is Required for Church Membership*. Nashville: B&H Publishing Group, 2015.

Jeon, Jeong Koo. *Biblical Theology: Covenants and the Kingdom of God in Redemptive History*. Eugene: Wipf & Stock, 2017.

Josephus, Flavius, Henry St J. Thackeray, and Flavius Josephus. *Books I-III*. Reprinted. Josephus Jewish Antiquities, 5 [1]. Cambridge: Harvard Univ. Press, 2001.

Kecmanović, Dušan. *The Mass Psychology of Ethnonationalism*. PATH in Psychology. New York: Plenum Press, 1996.

Kellner, Douglas. *Media Culture: Cultural Studies, Identity, and Politics between the Modern and the Postmodern*. London: Routledge, 1995.

Kent, Homer A. "The New Covenant And The Church," in *Grace Theological Journal*, 6.2, 1985.

Kirby, Alan. "The death of postmodernism and beyond." *Philosophy Now,* 58, 2006.

Koenig, John Franklin. *New Testament Hospitality: Partnership with Strangers as Promise and Mission*. Eugene: Wipf and Stock, 2001.

Koshul, Basit Bilal. *The Postmodern Significance of Max Weber's Legacy: Disenchanting Disenchantment*. New York: Palgrave Macmillan, 2005.

Leeman, Jonathan. *The Church and the Surprising Offense of God's Love: Reintroducing the Doctrines of Church Membership and Discipline*. IX Marks. Wheaton: Crossway Books, 2010.

Lenski, Gerhard. *The Religious Factor*. New York: Anchor Doubleday, 1963.

Lincoln, Andrew T., David A. Hubbard, Glenn W. Barker, Bruce Manning Metzger, and Andrew T. Lincoln. *Ephesians*. Nachdr. Word Biblical Commentary, [General ed.: David A. Hubbard; Glenn W. Barker. Old Testament ed.: John D. W. Watts. New Testament ed.: Ralph P. Martin]; Vol. 42. Waco: Word Books, 2005.

Longman, Tremper, and David E. Garland, eds. *The Expositor's Bible Commentary*. Rev. ed. Grand Rapids: Zondervan, 2006.

López, José, ed. *After Postmodernism: An Introduction to Critical Realism*. Reprinted. Continuum Studies in Critical Theory. London: Athlone Press, 2006.

Love, Rick. *GLOCAL: Following Jesus in the 21st Century*. Eugene: Cascade Books, 2017.

Lumpkin, William Latane, and Bill Leonard. *Baptist Confessions of Faith*. Valley Forge: Judson Press, 2011.

Lynch, Chloe. *Ecclesial Leadership as Friendship*. Explorations in Practical, Pastoral, and Empirical Theology. New York: Routledge, 2019.

Lyon, David. *Jesus in Disneyland: Religion in Postmodern Times*. Cambridge: Polity Press, 2000.

Matthews, Victor Harold, Bernard M Levinson, and Tikva Simone Frymer-Kensky. *Gender and Law in the Hebrew Bible and the Ancient Near East*. London: T & T Clark, 2004.

McGavran, Donald A., and C. Peter Wagner. *Understanding Church Growth*. Grand Rapids: W.B. Eerdmans, 1990.

McKean, Erin. *"Go Ahead, Make Up New Words!,"* TED Talks, 2014, accessed July 15, 2019, https://www.ted.com/talks/erin_mckean_go_ahead_make_up_new_words.

McKergow, Mark, and Helen L Bailey. *Host: Six New Roles of Engagement*. London: Solutions Books, 2014.

McLaughlin, Rebecca. *Confronting Christianity: 12 Hard Questions for the World's Largest Religion*. Wheaton: Crossway, 2019.

Morris, Helen. *Flexible Church: Being the Church in the Contemporary World*. London: SCM Press, 2019.

Moynagh, Michael. *Changing World, Changing Church: New Forms of Church, out-of-the-Pew Thinking, Initiatives That Work*. London: Monarch Books, 2003.

Moynagh, Michael, and Philip Harrold. *Church for Every Context: An Introduction to Theology and Practice*. London: SCM Press, 2012.

———. *Church for Every Context: An Introduction to Theology and Practice*. London: SCM Press, 2012.

Mugny, Gabriel, and Juan Antonio Pérez. *The Social Psychology of Minority Influence*. European Monographs in Social Psychology. Cambridge ; New York : Paris: Cambridge University Press ; Editions de la Maison des sciences de l'homme, 1991.

Murray, Stuart. *Church Planting: Laying Foundations*. North American ed. Scottdale, Pa: Herald Press, 2001.

Murray, Stuart (ed.), "Translocal Leadership: A Theological Reflection" in Translocal Ministry: 'equipping the churches for mission'. Didcot: The Baptist Union of Great Britain, 2004.

Novak, Michael. *Unmeltable Ethnics: Politics & Culture in American Life*. 2nd ed. New Brunswick: Transaction, 1996.

Nuttall, Geoffrey F. *Visible Saints: The Congregational Way, 1640-1660*. Oxford: Basil Blackwell, 1957.

Ott, Craig, and Harold A. Netland, eds. *Globalizing Theology: Belief and Practice in an Era of World Christianity*. Grand Rapids: Baker Academic, 2006.

OverviewBible. 'All The "One Another" Commands in the NT' accessed July 15, 2019, https://overviewbible.com/one-another-infographic/

Pagitt, Doug. *Church Re-Imagined: The Spiritual Formation of People in Communities of Faith*. Grand Rapids: Youth Specialties, 2005.

Payne, E.A. *Ways Known And To Be Made Known.* London: Baptist Union of Great Britain and Ireland, 1977.

Pearlman, Alison. *Smart Casual: The Transformation of Gourmet Restaurant Style in America*. Chicago: University of Chicago Press, 2013.

Pelikan, Jaroslav. *The Christian Tradition 5: Christian Doctrine and Modern Culture since 1700*. The Christian Tradition 5. Chicago: University of Chicago Press, 1989.

Peterson, Eugene. *Working The Angles: The Shape of Pastoral Integrity*. Grand Rapids: Eerdmans, 1987.

Pohl, Christine D. *Making Room: Recovering Hospitality as a Christian Tradition*. Grand Rapids: W.B. Eerdmans, 1999.

Putnam, Robert D. *Bowling Alone: The Collapse and Revival of American Community*. New York: Simon & Schuster, 2001.

Rah, Soong-Chan. *The next Evangelicalism: Releasing the Church from Western Cultural Captivity*. Downers Grove: IVP Books, 2009.

Renn, Stephen D., ed. *Expository Dictionary of Bible Words: Word Studies for Key English Bible Words Based on*

> *the Hebrew and Greek Texts*. Peabody: Hendrickson Publishers, 2005.

Reynolds, Geoffrey G, and Berkshire Baptist Association. *First among Equals.* Oxford: Berkshire, Southern and Oxfordshire and East Gloucestershire Baptist Associations., 1993.

Ritzer, George. *The McDonaldization of Society 5*. Los Angles: Pine Forge Press, 2008.

Root, Michael, and Risto Saarinen, eds. *Baptism and the Unity of the Church*. Grand Rapids: W.B. Eerdmans, 1998.

Sattler, Michael. 'The Schleitheim Confession of Faith' in *The Mennonite Quarterly Review*, XIX, 4, October 1945.

Sayers, Mark. Disappearing Church: From Cultural Relevance to Gospel Resilience. Chicago: Moody Publishers, 2016.

Schwartz, Barry. *The Paradox of Choice: Why More Is Less*. New York: Harper Perennial, 2007.

Shipley, C.E. The Baptists of Yorkshire, 1912, accessed June 29, 2019, https://files.huddersfield.exposed/localhistory/books/The%20Baptists%20of%20Yorkshire%20(1912)%20%5bLQ%20yale.39002085618248%5d.pdf

Smith, Gordon T. *A Holy Meal: The Lord's Supper in the Life of the Church*. Grand Rapids, Mich: Baker Academic, 2005.

Spang, Rebecca L. *The Invention of the Restaurant: Paris and Modern Gastronomic Culture*. Harvard Historical Studies 135. Cambridge: Harvard University Press, 2001.

Strong, James. *Strong's Exhaustive Concordance of the Bible*. Peabody: Hendrickson Pub., 2012.

Sweet, Leonard I. *AquaChurch 2.0: Piloting Your Church in Today's Fluid Culture*. Colorado Springs: David C Cook, 2008.

Sweet, Leonard I., Brian D. McLaren, and Jerry Haselmayer. *'A' Is for Abductive: The Language of the Emerging Church*. Grand Rapids: Zondervan, 2003.

Tajfel, Henri, ed. *Social Identity and Intergroup Relations*. European Studies in Social Psychology. Cambridge: Cambridge Univ. Press, 2010.

Taylor, Charles. *A Secular Age*. Harvard University Press, 2007.

Taylor, Nicholas. *Paul, Antioch, and Jerusalem: A Study in Relationships and Authority in Earliest Christianity*. Journal for the Study of the New Testament 66. Sheffield: JSOT Press, 1992.

Thackeray, Henry St J and Josephus Flavius, Books I-III, Reprinted, Josephus Jewish Antiquities, 5 [1]. Cambridge: Harvard Univ. Press, 2001.

Thomas, Richard. *Counting People In: Changing the Way We Think about Membership and the Church*. London: SPCK, 2003.

Trementozzi, David, and Amos Yong. *Salvation in the Flesh: Understanding How Embodiment Shapes Christian Faith*. Eugene: McMaster Divinity College Press, 2018.

UK Civil Society Almnac 2019, *'How Many People Volunteer and What Do They Do'* accessed July 15, 2019, https://data.ncvo.org.uk/volunteering/

Underhill, Edward Bean. *Records of a Church of Christ: Meeting in Broadmead, Bristol*. London: Forgotten Books, 2015.

Viola, Frank. *Reimagining Church: Pursuing the Dream of Organic Christianity*. Colorado Springs: David C. Cook, 2008.

Volf, Miroslav. *After Our Likeness: The Church as the Image of the Trinity*. Sacra Doctrina. Grand Rapids: William B. Eerdmans, 1998.

Ward, Peter. *Liquid Church.* Eugene: Wipf & Stock Publishers, 2013.

Weber, Max. *Ancient Judaism*. London: Collier Macmillan Publishers, 2014. http://www.myilibrary.com?id=899385.

Weinfield, Moshe. "The Covenant of Grant in the Old Testament and in the Ancient Near East," *Journal of the American Oriental Society,* 90, 1970.

White, B. R. *The English Baptists of the Seventeenth Century*. A History of the English Baptists, v. 1. London: Baptist Historical Society, 1983.

White, B. R., William H. Brackney, Paul S. Fiddes, and John H. Y. Briggs, eds. *Pilgrim Pathways: Essays in Baptist History in Honour of B.R. White*. Macon: Mercer University Press, 1999.

———, eds. *Pilgrim Pathways: Essays in Baptist History in Honour of B.R. White*. Macon: Mercer University Press, 1999.

Whitley, W.T. *The Works of John Smyth: Fellow of Christ's College, 1594-8,* Volume 1. Cambridge: Cambridge University Press, 1915.

Williamson, Paul R. *Sealed with an Oath: Covenant in God's Unfolding Purpose*. New Studies in Biblical Theology 23. Downers Grove: Apollos/InterVarsity Press, 2007.

Wollenberg, Anne. *'Image Problem Turn Recruits Away,'* The Guardian, citing the UK 2007-2008 Citizenship Survey, accessed July 15, 2019, https://www.theguardian.com/society/2008/sep/10/voluntarysector.volunteering

Wright, N. T. *Simply Jesus: Who He Was, What He Did, Why It Matters*. London: SPCK, 2011.
Wright, Nigel. *Challenge to Change*. Kingsway, 1991.
Zizioulas, Jean. *Being as Communion: Studies in Personhood and the Church*. London: Darton Longman & Todd, 2004.